It's a Long and Winding Road:
Finding Peace After My Struggle with Childhood Trauma

by Bonnie Dust

Dedication

**To my faithful, ever-working husband Roman Dust.
To my daughter Kristin Dust, a true gift from heaven.**

**Published by Richard McGuire Publishing,
Osoyoos, British Columbia, Canada.**

Editorial Advisor: Richard McGuire

www.richardmcguire.com

For permissions contact:

richard@richardmcguire.ca

ISBN: 978-1-9992367-1-7

Cover photo: Richard McGuire

Contents

Preface

Bonnie Dust first contacted me shortly after I left my job as editor of the *Osoyoos Times*. She'd written a book about her life and her struggle with mental health issues and she wanted help with publishing it.

I had no idea what to expect when I first drove to her farm north of Osoyoos to meet her. When I arrived, I met an intelligent woman who seemed very self-aware and had an important story to tell.

Not only was she lucid, but she recalled incidents from the past with remarkable detail.

She brought out a couple binders filled with her handwritten story, along with letters and various supporting information.

As I got to know her and learned more of her story, I also educated myself about some of the issues she raised.

Unfortunately, her experiences as a child abused by a neighbourhood pedophile and as an adult sexually exploited by her psychiatrist, happen more frequently than many realize.

Mental health issues too are more common than most of us know. Stigma and shame have silenced public discussion of both the impact that sexual predators have on their victims and on mental health in general.

Indeed, one in five Canadians experiences a mental illness or addiction in any given year, and by the time they are 40, half of all Canadians have had a mental illness. That's according to information cited by the Centre for Addiction and Mental Health (CAMH).

The most shocking part of Bonnie's experience was the inability of the mental health system to acknowledge that Bonnie's problems stemmed largely from childhood trauma. She tells of psychiatrists who had no interest in finding out about those traumas – their only solution was to fill her with antipsychotic and other drugs that left her as a zombie but did nothing to address the underlying issues.

There are, of course, some questions about the memories of a four-year-old child or an adult mental patient stupefied by antipsychotic drugs. Bonnie was clear when she couldn't remember details. It's possible her memory was faulty occasionally, but she tells the truth as she remembers it.

We decided it would serve no purpose to name some of the individuals involved. The pedophile died long ago, but he still has family. We did name her psychiatrist, Dr. Larry Anderson, who was convicted in a court of law for similar behaviour towards other patients.

My role has been to help Bonnie organize the material into a form that can be published as a book. I also interviewed her several times, adding what she told me to the manuscript she'd previously written.

There has been light editing, but most of the book is Bonnie's own words, either from the manuscript or the interviews. This is, after all, her story.

I hope you find her story as thought provoking as I did.

Richard McGuire

1. A Life with Misdiagnosis

It was July 1969 and the American astronauts were landing on the moon for the first time. I was 20 years old.

I'd gone several days without sleep, first partying on the coast where I was training to become a registered nurse, next attending a wedding party in Osoyoos, British Columbia, and then celebrating the moon landing at home, also in Osoyoos.

My mind was racing, and my body felt speeded up. My behaviour wasn't normal, but we were all having so much fun. Apparently, I talked about swimming across the lake and my friends tried to convince me not to and became worried.

A concerned friend called an ambulance. I was bundled by force into a straitjacket with plenty of ice packs on my arrival at St. Martin's Hospital in Oliver. It was a terrifying experience, which I have never forgotten.

Days later, I was taken to a psychiatric facility, the "Little Brown House," a two-storey house next to Kelowna General Hospital.

There, the psychiatrist in charge gave me antipsychotic medications and 30 electroconvulsive therapy treatments (ECTs), electric shocks. I became a complete vegetable, no longer remembering friends or even some of my family.

This time, my label was schizophrenia, a "fits everything" diagnosis often used in the 1960s to 1970s to describe most conditions.

I spent six months in the psychiatric unit. It was devastating. I lost my self-esteem and self-confidence. I felt slow, physically and emotionally. They didn't know that it was my spirit they were killing, not some terrible mental disease.

This wasn't my first misdiagnosis and it certainly wasn't the last. But it was the beginning of a life interrupted by periodic visits to hospital psychiatric wards, treated with drugs that made my condition worse, and labelled with different misdiagnoses, each carrying its own stigma.

Four years earlier, I had been misdiagnosed with hyperthyroidism. I was given an antithyroid medication and I missed the first two months of Grade 11.

Ten years later, an endocrine specialist did tests that indicated my thyroid was normal and always had been!

But the misdiagnosis that followed me throughout my life was bipolar disorder. I was given the label "manic-depressive," as it was then called, in 1974 at the psych ward in Penticton.

After being labelled "schizophrenic" for five years, suddenly I was "bipolar" instead. It didn't seem to matter to psychiatrists that I wasn't displaying many of the bipolar symptoms, such as periods of depression. Over the years, I've met numerous patients with real bipolar disorder, and they had much bigger problems than mine.

Never did psychiatrists attempt to understand or even ask about my underlying emotional problems. One time when I tried to talk to a psychiatrist about childhood trauma, he shut me down, telling me he didn't do psychology.

It was as though the mental health professionals operated in their own little silos, unable to consider other possibilities. Too often, the solution was to prescribe antipsychotic medications. If those didn't achieve the desired results, they just increased the dosage until I became like a zombie.

Doctors often forget that patients have feelings and are tuned in to what they are going through. Rather than asking patients how they felt, it was easier just to prescribe pills, forgetting that those medications might not be doing us any good at all.

Never was I given the opportunity to sit with a doctor and discuss how I really felt, how things were working at home, whether I was happy or sad. Never did they ask what was happening in my life in the week before my hospitalization. During the years when I had mental health counselling, there seemed to be no communication between the counsellors and the doctors.

The stigmas left by these misdiagnoses were destructive in their own way. The schizophrenia diagnosis was the worst. If you tell people you're a schizophrenic, they're not going to want to be your friend. I lost a lot of friends when I told people I was diagnosed as schizophrenic. Being overmedicated and going through electric shock treatments until you're brain-dead made it worse.

In contrast, the stigmas of being labelled with hyperthyroidism or bipolar disorder were less likely to turn away friends, but they had consequences, nonetheless.

When I was diagnosed and medicated for hyperthyroidism, I became fat, blown up and brain-dead. I went from being a top student to failing almost every subject as I tried to finish grades 11 and 12. I lost confidence and barely scraped through.

When I was branded as bipolar, I was suspected of having manic episodes if I acted too cheerful or even dressed well. Spending money could set off alarm bells for those around me.

I noticed that the times I became speeded up tended to occur in the late spring and early summer when the farm work was more stressful.

The cookie-cutter solution for someone labelled as bipolar was to drug them to keep them from getting too high or too low. There was never any education provided to the patient so they could understand and cope with the condition.

As someone branded as bipolar, I was in and out of psych wards, often physically pinned down and forcibly administered medications. It was always about controlling the patient rather than listening and collaborating to help them get better.

My situation improved when my medications were reduced or phased out. For almost 20 years, from 1979 to 1999, I managed to avoid psychiatrists and I did well on a very low dose of Lithium.

During those years, I gained a better understanding of the causes of my condition. Some of it was hormonal. I began experiencing symptoms of menopause early, in my late 30s. This explained some of my temperature problems and drastic mood changes.

I observed that the triggers preceding anxiety attacks were often minor traumas that set me over the edge. If a person is going fast and is in fight or flight response, it doesn't necessarily mean they are manic, as the doctors assumed. Rather, it could be the result of a traumatic event or maybe stress in their life at the time.

It was not until I was about 35 in the mid-1980s that I began to understand the connection between childhood trauma and what I was experiencing as an adult.

Post-traumatic stress disorder (PTSD) has only been understood in recent years. When I was around 35, a mental health counsellor became convinced that I had PTSD after I told him about a few of my childhood experiences.

Over the years, mental health counsellors determined that I had emotional problems, but they didn't accept my label of bipolar. In fact, never once did I have a counsellor treat me as bipolar, as the psychiatrists insisted.

Only in January 2002, did a new psychiatrist, well trained in PTSD, confirm that this, and not bipolar disorder, was the cause of my problems. I finally began to feel confident that we were getting to the root of my lifelong condition.

He subsequently moved on and my earlier bipolar misdiagnosis returned to haunt me. But I learned to become my own advocate, to become informed and to take charge of my treatment.

My lifelong journey from childhood trauma to psychiatric hell and ultimately to self-discovery and peace with myself is outlined in the following chapters.

I hope that you can learn from my long and winding road and that my experience empowers you to take charge of your own wellness.

2. Beginnings

I was born Bonnie Joan Hesketh. My parents were Freda and Harry Hesketh. It was January 28, 1949 in the Oliver St. Martins Hospital.

It was an extremely cold winter. Mom and Dad were having the house built on their undeveloped property north of Osoyoos, British Columbia.

The farmland reached down to the shores of the north basin of Osoyoos Lake, a long lake fed by the Okanagan River. Across the lake, we looked up at rugged mountains, their rocky surfaces dotted with evergreens.

Down the lake to the south sits the present town of Osoyoos. When I was born, it was a village of fewer than 1,000 people. Today it is a town of more than 5,000. Osoyoos was built around a lake crossing on a long spit with a bridge that separated the lake's north and south basins.

Farther south, the lake extends into the United States. There, at its southern end, lies Oroville, Washington, with about 1,500 people in my childhood and only slightly bigger today.

Oroville was part of our lives growing up. We went down for movies and dances and some of us had American boyfriends.

The land is dry, desert-like, with antelope brush, sagebrush and cacti. Over the decades, thanks to the lake and river, it's been turned to lush irrigated farmland with orchards and more recently vineyards.

My parents moved to Osoyoos in 1946. It was the end of World War II and Dad's experience as a prisoner of war in Germany. Dad was a navigator in the Canadian Air Force. His plane was shot down in a bombing attack over Berlin. On return to Canada, Dad was a walking skeleton, nearly blind and had lost all his teeth.

My dad, Harry Hope Hesketh, was born October 18, 1911. He died at 93 years on January 1, 2005.

Dad walked one and a half miles to school in Bienfait in southeastern Saskatchewan. He took grades 3 to 8. At 16, he started working in a bank. He was 28 when he joined the Air Force.

He loved all sports. He was good at baseball, swimming, curling and especially tennis.

As a young man, he even owned a Harley-Davidson. My two brothers each ended up with the same brand of motorcycle.

On Dad's side, his parents were Beatrice Hope, born in Ireland, and Harry Hesketh Sr., born in England. They lived on a farm in Bienfait. Grandpa worked in a coal mine at nearby Shand. They raised seven children along with cows, chickens and workhorses.

My mother was born Elfreda Beryl Fowler on April 5, 1920 and she died January 24, 2015.

Mom's parents lived on a farm at Fillmore, Saskatchewan. They had wheat and other grain crops.

Grandma Florence was born in Manitoba. Grandpa Jim Fowler was from Iowa. There were five children. Mom's brother, Murray, was killed in a farming accident at about 10 years of age.

Mom and Dad married in 1942 in Saskatchewan during the Second World War. When Dad went overseas, Mom joined the Women's Army Corps. She did supply inspection all over Saskatchewan.

In later years, Grandma and Grandpa Hesketh moved to Osoyoos. They lived in the first home east of Legion Beach. They had a huge garden. When Grandma died, all the family were at the house with her. We were all stressed out. I came out with the "F" word and Dad heard me. I was hauled to the sink and my mouth thoroughly washed with soap.

Grandpa later moved out to live with us on the farm. He was such a great gardener and painter. He also played the harmonica. Grandpa grew hollyhocks, iris, and tiger lilies, which grow still over a large area.

Due to a mining accident, Grandpa's back was injured. His back remained a large "hump." It didn't stop him from working hard.

We had plenty of fresh strawberries, corn and potatoes.

When Mom could no longer cope with raising three children, looking after Grandpa and working, things had to change. Grandpa became a resident of the first Sunnybank seniors' home in Oliver in the 1960s.

I received a few traits from Grandpa that I am grateful for, especially creativity and gardening.

I moved into his bedroom when he went to Oliver. It was heaven to have my own space.

Grandma and Grandpa Fowler came out to Osoyoos in the fall of 1948 and much of 1949. Grandpa Jim and his son Allan started to build our family home out on the farmland. The winter was severe, so they had to build a garage with a wood stove first. The home was very well built, and the main structure has never been changed.

Grandma and Grandpa Fowler usually drove to Osoyoos to visit. They helped out when Mom had us three kids. Gerry was born in 1948 and I was born in 1949. Laurie was four years later. My parents lived in town until the house was complete.

We went to visit our relatives in Saskatchewan often by car or train. We got on in Salmon Arm and off in Regina. The train was exciting and fun, especially the tunnels. The views of the snow-covered Rockies were amazing.

In my teens, my cousin Karen from Fillmore and I took the train from Regina to Salmon Arm. That was a very fun trip. Karen and I had such a great friendship.

My grandparents later built a home in downtown Fillmore. Grandma was happy to be off the farm. She used to type me letters about everything she did in a day. Canning fruit and berries during the summer, bread, buns and pies all through the year. In the fall she helped prepare meals for harvest crews.

I had a great-grandmother who lived nearby in Fillmore. Grandma Fowler was her daughter. My great-grandmother was Drusilla Hunter. She was very short and lived in a very tiny house. I enjoyed visiting her. She lived alone until the age of 102! I wish I knew more about her.

Grandpa Jim did wonderful woodworking. He made me a "Hope Chest," which I filled with secret treasures. Later I used it for all my art supplies. Now I have my daughter's treasures in it. It was a gift from the heart, and it will last my lifetime.

Harry Hope Hesketh, the author's father.

My Grandma Fowler died first with heart problems in 1964. Grandpa Jim died in the fall of 1972, also with a heart issue. I was very sad and missed my visits with him in Fillmore.

When Mom and Dad married in 1942, my dad was posted overseas the same day. They only had a few days to spend together. Men flew to Eastern Canada, then by boat to England, in very rough sea.

Dad was a navigator in a Lancaster bomber. Flying over Berlin, they could only see thick smoke. They did not see guns shooting up at them. When their bomber was hit, they grabbed personal bags then parachuted out into darkness.

Dad had to jump first as the navigator sat at the bottom of the plane. Luckily, they all survived except the rear gunner.

They first tried to run and hide in the countryside. They were not safe long. The Germans found Dad and he was put in a POW camp. It was Stalag Luft III in Lower Silesia, now in Poland. The prison camp was 100 miles southeast of Berlin, holding 10,000 inmates.

Men in the service were trained to deny how terrible the conditions were. The men got one cup of water a day and a piece of bread on rare occasions. Dad wrote home when able and kept a logbook, which is a treasure. He had done sketches in it and many "tall tales" of their good life in prison camp.

Many letters went back-and-forth. Mom sent care parcels and the Red Cross sent special shipments of food and cigarettes to the POW camps.

Mom and her brother Allan were in the Army. Mom's job was to inspect all Army supplies used in World War II. She covered the province of Saskatchewan.

In January 1945, prisoners saw freedom as World War II was winding down and the Soviets liberated the POW camp. Dad, along with thousands of others, had to walk out of Germany to the coast of France. They boarded ships to Eastern Canada. From there they took trains to get home.

Dad and Mom had to leave for Vancouver after visiting family. Dad had medical help with his loss of vision. Shaughnessy Hospital was for the war veterans. He was so frail and malnourished. They did surgery

Elfreda Beryl Hesketh (nee Fowler), the author's mother.

on his eyes. Pneumonia and bouts of pleurisy were frequent for many years.

When Dad worked in the bank, he boarded with Chuck Emery's family in Saskatchewan. He knew Chuck had an aunt in Penticton. She directed my parents to Osoyoos to find Chuck running Emery Motors.

Mom and Dad moved to Osoyoos in January 1946. The population was approximately 400. It was the year Osoyoos became a village municipality. For the first month, they rented a unit at the Osoyoos Motel on the north side of Main Street.

In May 1946, Mom and Dad bought the post office building from George Carlson. Dad became the new postmaster. Until Dad's health and eyes improved, Mom did the majority of the work. For several years, "home" was at the back and basement of this building.

3. Starting to Farm in the Desert

Mom and Dad bought farmland in 1947, under the VLA (Veterans Land Act). It was barren except for desert plants and billions of rocks. It was neither sandy soil nor fertile. To the east it bordered the lake. Getting water for domestic use and irrigation was a priority.

Dad was also postmaster in Osoyoos for 25 years. Mom worked alongside Dad either full or part-time.

"Capistrano Heights" is what my dad named our farm. Down below on the bank of clay, the swallows came to nest.

I was six months old when we moved out to our new home. As my brother and I got older, we could play outside. I had a walker and he had a small tricycle. We would push our way across gravel and rocks. Because we were only 11 months apart, Mom said we were called "Irish twins."

My dad built a pumphouse at the lake. It had to force water up a very steep bank. The water was piped to a cistern next to the house. It was a huge concrete underground structure. It could be filled as needed, except during winter months. We learned to ration water. Baths were once a week and "sponge baths" more practical.

Irrigation water was very important in starting any growth of vegetation, ground crops, or fruit trees. It took years to figure out a good system of above ground pipes. They were aluminum pipe in long sections which joined together. One upright sprinkler head was on each pipe.

Before sprinklers were brought in, people had ditch irrigation. Mom and Dad had raised ground crops this way, between plantings of young apple trees.

Dad seeded alfalfa and clover and different grasses to help hold the moisture in the soil. For every hole dug, there would be a wheelbarrow full of rocks.

Dad planted a variety of trees. We had red and golden delicious, Winesap, McIntosh and crabapples for pollinating. We also had cherries, Italian prunes, peaches and apricots.

During peak season we all helped on the farm. Even as preschoolers, we helped pick up rocks and prunings. They had to be loaded into a trailer and hauled away.

In the spring of 1950, Dad seeded lawn grass, and it was growing nicely by summer. A privet hedge was planted around the house and lawn as a border. Siberian elms provided some shade eventually.

Many of these elms grew on the bank sloping down towards the lake. Cottonwood, poplars, sandbar willow, Oregon grape, wild Nootka roses, sumac, snowberry, and poison ivy were abundant closer to the lake. One very tall ponderosa pine is still standing today. Edible berries were Saskatoon and chokecherry. This habitat all remains in its natural state.

The Canadian Pacific Railway (CPR) line cut through the property between two lots. We had a private crossing. The train went by several times a day, hauling fruit or supplies to and from Osoyoos.

The farm work had to be done early in the morning, evenings or weekends. The post office was keeping my parents busy on weekdays.

My two brothers and I slept in our full-size basement. Both upstairs and down had a fireplace.

At one end, my father created a large electric train layout. There were mountains, tunnels, stations and trees etc. Everything was on a raised area about two and a half feet off the floor. We had many years of enjoyment, especially through the winters.

In the warmer months, we would be outside with our parents, friends or over at the neighbours. Visitors came in summer months, sometimes aunts, uncles and cousins. Mom had a lot of extra cooking to do.

One hobby Dad enjoyed for a number of years was that of a beekeeper. He had enough hives to do our orchard. The bees loved the clover. We loved the honey, especially chunks of waxy honeycomb to chew on.

Elfreda holds Bonnie and Harry holds her brother Gerald at Easter 1950.

Dad built two big structures to the north. One was for raising chickens and turkeys. The other building was possibly a type of greenhouse.

Baby chicks were hatched in our own basement. Skunks and neighbouring dogs killed many chickens. The turkeys flew over to neighbours' roofs, getting a few farmers upset. We helped feed the chickens and gather eggs.

As the farm progressed, we had more and more animals. Our first dog was Lady, a beautiful Irish setter. One cat had kittens and then cats were plenty. They provided control of the mice.

I became a horse lover about 10 years of age. "Epona" was my first horse, a purebred Arab not completely broken. It was a big error in judgment. Dad had to return her.

One late night Frank Smith sold us "Blackey." He was old, lame with ring bone and ever so gentle. He was an excellent starter horse for me. I learned how to feed and care for him.

Years later, Blackey was sold back to Frank Smith. Dad bought me "Kitten," a purebred Tennessee Walker. She was just a young filly so needed a lot of training.

About the same time Frank Smith found us Heidi. She was a gentle cattle horse. My older brother Gerry rode her most of the time. We did rides all over Osoyoos and surrounding hills.

Dad thrived on being busy. Next thing he was into buying and selling feeder steers. The property was fenced off with concrete posts and barbed wire. Down over the bank he constructed a large feeding station. It was an amazing set up. Bales of hay could be put on a conveyor belt up to the top where they could be stored.

Nearby there was a huge chute for delivering apple pulp from up top, down into a feeding trough. The cattle got a little tipsy on apple pulp.

Often the cattle and horses grazed in the orchard. The horses liked to eat cherries and apples. We had to be diligent in closing gates going to and from our property. Our dog would help herd the cattle.

In earlier days, fruit was picked into wooden boxes. They held approximately 40 pounds. It was much more work as each box had to be moved about by hand. They had to be delivered by truck or trailer to the packinghouse.

Dad built us a boat, fiberglass and all. We did all kinds of boating and eventually waterskiing. Dad was an extremely clever fellow! All the neighbourhood kids got to come and swim or ski. We were very lucky children.

Dad was also involved with the village council and Osoyoos Credit Union. Mom and Dad curled at the old rink, which later became the museum. They also played bridge and other social events were important to them.

Bonnie, right, is pictured with her older brother Gerald and younger brother Laurence, c. 1953.

Everyone smoked post-World War II it seemed. I found it difficult being in a smoke-filled environment.

Mom said I was a handful at birth. I was colicky and cried much of the time. Both my older brother and I arrived at eight months, not full-term.

As toddlers, we became healthier and played well together. Dad and Mom had wooden cars, wagons and sprinklers for us to play in. In winter we got sleigh rides.

There was no preschool. Grade 1 was in the primary section. The Osoyoos Elementary and Junior High went up to grade 10. It was all one big school. We had a big gym and cafeteria.

I loved printing and art. Other subjects became difficult – anything to do with math, adding, subtracting etc.

We took the bus most days unless we were to go to the post office after school. Sometimes our bus stop had up to 10 or more children. We were all good friends.

Mom got me into dancing lessons at a young age of four or five. I took lessons in Scottish dancing, folk, ballet, toe and tap. Many of my friends took dancing also. Once or twice a year there was a concert put on for family members. Mom was so busy making costumes. I'm still dancing at 70. I can thank my mom for this wonderful lifetime gift.

At some point I joined Brownies along with other friends. It was a large group with many fun activities. We met weekly after school and attended social events.

Lunch time at the school was special. Mrs. Pugh ran a wonderful meal program. Along with a hot meal, ice cream treats and milk were available. Friday was fish and fries.

At recess and lunch time, we played games on the smooth concrete floor. Otherwise we went outside. There were many games. I loved jacks, lacrosse ball, tetherball, skipping and hopscotch. It was a good break from classroom stress.

Mom took many photos, making albums for all three of us. Christmas was fun for a few years, then became more and more stressful.

At 11 months, I received my first doll. She had long blonde hair and eyes that moved. My Grandma Fowler made clothes for her and mailed them to me. My daughter, then granddaughter have enjoyed my doll.

Birthday parties were a big event. Mom really knew how to put on a party for us. Everyone dressed up and received hats and noisemakers. The banana cakes were great, three layers with banana slices in between.

I was 12 before we got a TV, one of the first in our neighbourhood. That was a new negative distraction for us. Up until then, our time was full of creativity and imagination. We never lacked things to do.

Dad was very strict, teaching us good manners. We had to eat everything put in front of us. There was no junk food around to spoil our appetites. Mom made very healthy suppers.

Mealtime could get very hostile. Dad would go after us with a leather belt and we would try and hide in a small space where he couldn't reach us.

Dad had anger and rages for many years. He wrestled with demons from his past at a time when post-traumatic stress disorder (PTSD) was not understood.

He was raped by a Catholic priest in Saskatchewan when he was an altar boy. Later, as an adolescent, he was raped by a Boy Scout leader.

Only in his 80s, was he was able to tell me the truth about the German prison camp. I was probably the first one he ever told about what happened to him. I began to understand how these traumas affected him and it brought us closer.

But growing up, the environment was stressful as my parents fought and my father beat my mother. She would grab her car keys, slam the door and drive away for hours. I never knew if she was in a crash somewhere.

When my parents had a big fight, my mom fought back, and the situation escalated. I spent a lot of nights not sleeping because I would hear them fighting and screaming. The next morning, she would be covered in bruises.

My mom resented a lot of what my dad did and his behaviour was out of control at times. He drank, engaged in risky behaviour and spent money on things he didn't need.

My dad was a very intelligent man, but he could be impulsive, sometimes putting other people and himself at risk.

On the surface, he was an upstanding member of the community, running the post office for 25 years, starting the first credit union and serving on village council.

He was sharp with numbers and could add anything in his head at a time before calculators and computers. He did tree grafting, building projects and repairs. He was hyperactive and busy all the time.

As he got older, he slowed down and mellowed, but he could still be inappropriate and offensive.

In later years, I was able to forgive my father for his behaviour, anger, fighting with mom, and heavy discipline towards us three kids. Things may have been very different if people had known more about PTSD back in World War I and World War II.

4. The Secret

At first it seemed our rural neighbourhood was a nice one with mixed nationalities. People got along and often helped each other out.

Nearby, there was an elderly couple I didn't like. They never spoke English and I believe they communicated in German.

The man used to try to lure children to his work shed with offers of candy. Every child became a target of this evil man.

Because most parents worked, children were left unprotected or were left with neighbours. The elderly couple sometimes babysat us. The man worked with machinery and often had access to neighbourhood garages where he did work.

I was about four years old when I had my first encounters with him, and my younger brother was just a baby.

Some of my recollections have faded with time, but some are as vivid as the day they happened.

I remember the man and his wife babysitting us. He would sit in the living room and pull his penis out of his pants, rubbing and scratching it until it was bleeding. All the time, his wife just watched.

He was old, ugly and always chuckling. I didn't understand that something was wrong until much later, but he made me feel sick.

My strongest memory, from around the same time, was being confined in his shed. It was a machinist shed with lots of equipment for his work. Even at the time, in the early 1950s, the wooden shed seemed old and dilapidated. It probably dated back to the 1930s.

Inside the shed was a big potbellied wood stove. A fire burned inside, and long-handled pokers sat heating in the stove.

There was a big bolt on the shed's door. There was no way for a small child to escape.

My older brother was with me, along with a neighbour boy.

For years afterwards, I experienced flashbacks. I remember we were stripped from the waist down and the old man was putting the pokers into the fire and then sticking them out toward us. I guess he was indicating that if we didn't take off our clothes, he would touch us with the hot iron.

I don't remember exactly how he communicated with us since he didn't speak English, but he must have somehow indicated what he wanted.

The shed was full of blue-grey smoke and had a strong smell. I was terrified of the fire, knowing this man had complete control over us. That image is etched into my mind.

I don't recall that he actually touched me, though I think there were times when he tried. Nor do I remember if he played with his penis when he had us in his shed as he did while babysitting. All I remember is the sheer terror of being confined to that shed with the burning fire and the hot pokers that he brandished.

I started having nightmares as a young child and would awake cold with sweat, too frightened to move. When I was much older, I had daytime flashbacks, thinking of that stove and the pokers.

It was only as an adult that I learned the word for people like this man was "pedophile." He never forced me to have sex with him, but I found out years later that he performed oral sex on the neighbourhood boys when he was abusing them.

A few years after the shed experiences, I remember him getting me and my friend to climb ladders and then he poked around underneath our clothing.

He seemed to be really enjoying himself around us. I think part of being a pedophile is they get off on the power of the fear that they instill in the children they affect.

Some people have tried to suggest that the fact he never actually raped me meant nothing serious happened. But that's foolish thinking.

Small children don't have a choice when they're abused or controlled by an adult or older person. Definitely there are many things that will affect a child that have nothing to do with actual intercourse.

The pedophile was often around and just having him in my presence made me fearful.

His shed continued to traumatize me for years. I'm told that as a child I used to run whenever I passed it. It haunted me into adulthood.

5. Growing Up

Mrs. Emmy Meronek was my teacher in grade 4. Something very special happened that year.

Our teacher got in touch with a grade 4 teacher in Grimsby, Lincolnshire, England. We were matched up with an English student, and soon after, letters were being sent back and forth.

My penpal is Linda Brown. We corresponded several times a year, especially birthdays and Christmas. Linda became a teacher. She had extremely neat printing and writing.

We remained in contact for many years.

In May 1988, I visited Linda and her husband John at their home in Banstead, Surrey, England. It was a great experience to fly by myself to Gatwick Airport. I met their son Paul and daughter Kerry.

Linda and I had married and had our daughters at similar times. We had a great visit and exciting day trips. Many pictures to treasure!

My grade 6 teacher was Al Whiteford from Australia. He was a dark, handsome man. I loved his class and learning about Australia. He was the basketball coach for the girls' rep team for grades 7, 8 and 9. After school and on weekends he taught tennis for free at the community park. I played tennis for many years.

Ivy Norcross was one of my teachers in grade 7 and became my tutor in grade 11. Years later, as a nurse, I did home care for her.

Hank Petersen was my teacher in grades 9 and 10. He recognized that I had major emotional problems that were causing my marks to deteriorate.

In earlier grades, I was always near the top of my class. By the end of grade 10, I was very much at the bottom of the class and the teachers were trying to figure out what was wrong.

I babysat for the Petersens and he would ask me about what was going on in my life. I became friends with his wife, who had six kids. She knew I had problems and couldn't talk to my parents.

Bill MacLeod was our excellent principal.

In grades 7, 8 and 9, I played basketball. I joined the track team and enjoyed high jump, broad jump, relay and shotput. I couldn't handle the shower room or change room after physical education or sports. I practised avoidance big time. I wasn't like my classmates; I was so skinny. I wasn't developing like the other girls.

At lunch time we played chess in a classroom. If we had money, we could go to the "Ice Berg" occasionally for a treat or lunch. It was the first fast food place, run by Mr. and Mrs. Fields.

My mother was able to sew a dress for our first school dance. Years of costume making and now clothes for school.

We also had a school band. I was to play the clarinet. I wasn't musical and never understood the music books. It just became an added stress.

One activity our family did together was downhill skiing. The ski hill was called "Borderline." It was on a north slope off Highway 3, just east of Anarchist Mountain. It started as a rope tow and later a T-bar was constructed.

If our parents were busy, Alfred Gruhl took us to ski in his Volkswagen van. We would sleep all the way home. He was a very kind man to do this for us.

Mom and her friend Dag Jones went to Mount Baldy to ski for many of their senior years. I eventually switched over to cross country, enjoying many years of it with my husband and daughter.

I took on more and more responsibilities as I got into junior high. I was the president of the students' council, patrol leader, then company leader in Girl Guides. I became a much-needed babysitter for the Petersen family of six children. I belonged to the Blue Sage Riders and went in horse shows around the South Okanagan. Another job was janitor for the post office.

In Girl Guides I was working on my "All-Around Cord." On Saturdays I cleaned the house for Mom.

Bonnie in Girl Guides, about 1963.

My marks were good in grades 8 and 9, but in grade 10 there was a sudden change. With stress in my life and emerging health problems, I began to struggle, failing in four subjects.

On Awards Day at school, I somehow managed to receive three or four awards despite my failing grades.

In July 1964, I attended the Girl Guide Heritage Camp in Prince Edward Island.

The following summer I got to take the train to Saskatchewan to visit Grandpa Jim and cousin Karen. After 10 days, Karen and I came back to Osoyoos. I babysat the rest of the summer. Things were busy.

Brownies was the first large group I belonged to. There were many of us and it was very popular. After several years we advanced to Girl Guides, "flying up" as it was called.

Girl Guides was a bit like the Army. We had a captain, lieutenant, company leader, patrol leaders and a lot of rules. Our meetings were well run by Dot Lewis, Louise Abel, and Dolly Waterman. Girl Guides taught me what I know today. I often explain to people it was my only practical education.

Girl Guides taught us how to be safe and have fun camping in the wild. We learned to be creative, industrious and content with roughing it.

I've learned to observe what is around me. In Girl Guides, we had to know all the wildflowers and trees. We had to do a trackers badge, going up into the mountains and making plaster casts of cougar tracks.

Guides was structured and there were many rules to follow. We had to learn so much, but it was very practical, and it stays with you the rest of your life.

We were the busiest young girls in Osoyoos. We had day hikes, weekend camps, summer camps, bake sales, exchange visits with Grand Coulee Dam Girl Scouts and Christmas parties. It was exciting and fun. Girl Guides was a challenge and the discipline was what really paid off.

First, to belong we had to attend meetings for at least one month. You then did the tenderfoot test. If you passed, you then became enrolled as a Guide.

After passing the tenderfoot test, it was on to second class. This included nature intelligence, safety, crafts, health and service. It was all a hands-on learning experience. In the '50s and '60s, Girl Guides were older than Guides today. We were teenagers. I'm sure we drove our leaders right up the wall at times. What a responsibility they had!

To move forward to first class, we were expected to retain all previous knowledge that we had gained so far. We also had to have a minimum of one weekend camping at a Girl Guides camp.

We had to read and learn the history of guiding. We learned how to use a compass, read and follow a map. We did cooking and sewing. We learned to care for others and ourselves in danger and sickness. Care of children was included.

Girl Guides was a reward system. We were rewarded with precious badges for our accomplishments. Later we could move forward to obtain higher awards. I became a dedicated Guide, later earning my All-Around Cord, then the highest attainment, the Gold Cord. We were presented with our gold cords in Victoria at Government House. By that time I was a Land Ranger. Our Land Ranger group was a smaller group in senior high school.

Guide camps were a great experience we all enjoyed. Every night we had a campfire, all sitting in a cozy circle. We took turns organizing the evening entertainment. I loved the songs, but had much difficulty singing. Luckily, we had some very good singers in our group, and they could get us through. The skits were hilarious.

Our tents were huge. The long "ridge" pole was supported by the "A" poles at either end. We had to dig rain trenches for the sides of the tent to drain water into. Flaps went up during the day for ventilation. We had daily patrol and tent inspection.

Patrol leaders camp was often at Johnstone Creek, the May long weekend. We were the older girls, but often got into the most trouble. One night our tent was raided by older boys. I had a major panic attack. As it turned out, the fellows were boyfriends of girls from Grand Forks. No harm done – just a lot of screaming and confusion. It was common to have our nights disrupted by someone taking ill, noises, spooky stories or suspicious shadows lurking about.

Camp wasn't for sissies. You had to be healthy and motivated. The cooking was usually done over open fires. There were the odd accidental burns and spills. We had to heat our dish water even. Sometimes we had to build our own biffies or outdoor washrooms! They were unique, walls of fir bows, sturdy construction out of limbs of trees, and a washbasin with Dettol and water to wash up on exit.

The highlight of my guiding was in July 1964, when I was 15 years old. Heritage camps were being held all across Canada. I was one of the top two girl guides of B.C., which allowed me the choice of which province I'd like to attend camp in. I chose P.E.I. It was a two-week camp at Brackley Beach. It was a three-day trip by air to get there! It was also my first time flying! We had to do it alone, without adults to accompany us. I must've touched down in every major airport between Penticton and New Brunswick. Some stopovers were up to 10 hours long. Our baggage was sent straight through, so we only had a few things in a small carry-on. Three days in the same clothes, three days without sleep. Our last flight was in a three-seater over to P.E.I. from Fredericton.

I took slides of the trip so I could share them later. We had a wonderful time, after the rain stopped. Just about every tent got flooded out the first two days. Some sleeping bags were saturated!

The entire two weeks were packed with exciting adventures. We were guests of the city of Charlottetown at a civic luncheon at the Charlottetown Hotel. We visited the Confederation chamber at the provincial building. Later we were guests of the provincial government for dinner at the hotel again. I was asked to sit at the head table. Now that made me very nervous. I was honoured to sit beside the mayor and other dignitaries.

Later that evening we went to "sulky" driven horse races. Camp was an hour's drive away from Charlottetown. Sometimes we went by car and other times on a bus.

One day we crossed the Northumberland Strait on the MV Abegweit ship. There was a big lobster carnival in Summerside. On the way home we visited the "Woodleigh" replicas and Anne of Green Gables.

When I returned to Osoyoos, I felt a little strange. It had been almost three weeks of excitement and not much sleep. I went back to my babysitting job, janitor job at the post office, my horses, helping Mom at home and Dad in the orchard. I must express my gratitude to all my Girl Guide leaders from the early days! They were all very dedicated and devoted a big part of their lives to be our leaders. We were not always on our best behaviour.

I appreciated all the support from my fellow Girl Guides and leaders when achieving the first Gold Cord in Osoyoos.

Of girls in my grade, I was one of the first to get my own horse. Then Judy, Leslie and Margaret. Later Moni next door rode our horses until she got her own.

Gail, Heather and Susan, a grade ahead of us, were into horses as well.

We had a well-run riding club in Osoyoos called the "Blue Sage Riders." There were meetings, local club horse shows and out-of-town shows. Most of the events were Western: barrel race, pole bending, relays, broad jump etc.

Moni could ride Kitten in junior events and won many ribbons. I rode in intermediate and adult events.

One year, Susan and I were Princesses and Heather Queen. The next year I was Queen alone. Our outfits were very pretty blue flower print Western shirts with a plain blue vest and pants.

We were in parades, including Cherry Carnival, either in a convertible or on horseback for horse show openings. We went to places in the South Okanagan including Penticton and Summerland.

The Blue Sage Riders was an active club. We met once a month and had a horse show at least once a year.

Kitten and I were accident-prone. In Princeton I was hurt in a relay. You had to ride down, jump off, and go through a barrel. I got off too close hitting the sharp barrel edge and cutting my leg. It was off to the hospital for stitches.

In Summerland, they had just watered the track down to settle the dust. Kitten slipped and fell, throwing me. I was knocked unconscious for a short while.

Kitten, being a purebred, was a very high-strung horse. She spooked easily and things got her overly excited.

Bonnie barrel races at the Blue Sage Riders horse show in September 1967.

One time a piece of paper blew across in front of us as I rode at the edge of the orchard. She took off at high speed knocking me off, going under a large apple tree. Mr. Van Duzee came along in his car and saw me lying in the grass unconscious. Apparently, he carried me all the way to the house. One of my parents then took me to see Dr. Sheppard. I had a concussion.

The Wagon Wheel Ranch had horses to rent years ago. I was about 10 when we'd go up in the summer to ride. If there was a circus in town, they sometimes had Shetland ponies for kids to ride. I was maybe three or four sitting on my first horses. When I gave up my horse at age 20, I never went back to riding again. I did miss the long rides up in the mountains around Osoyoos. Moni, my girlfriend next door, and I had so much fun riding together.

6. Health Problems

My grade 8 and 9 marks remained very good. By grade 10 there was a sudden change. It was our last year in Osoyoos junior high. I was failing four subjects. I barely made it, and had many teachers concerned about my decline in health along with my grades.

I had difficulties dealing with all kinds of stress, especially emotional and mental.

I was very tired and often fell asleep in class. My back and neck caused many problems. Mom was first told my back was broken and I'd have to be put in a body cast. Next, I was sent to specialists in Vancouver. They said my spine had not developed properly from birth. They told me to take calcium supplements.

Another complication in my life was my American boyfriend. Mike was from Oroville and we ended up going steady. I became emotionally upset frequently.

I met Mike at a big dance in Oroville when I was in grade 10. Several of my friends at the dance also found American boyfriends and one girl ended up marrying hers. We didn't like the Canadian boys that much because they were our age and the American boys we met were a year older.

Mike gave me a ring that looked like a huge diamond but was actually crystal. People teased me about it. He played guitar and was in a country music band called the Mustangs.

He had a motorcycle and I spent a lot of time going back and forth with him on the bike between Osoyoos and Oroville.

But Mike was unreliable. He made a lot of dates and never showed or would show up several hours later. He always had an excuse. My parents pressured me to break up with him because he always left me waiting around.

Our relationship was a continuous roller coaster. The boys in grade 11 at my new school in Oliver constantly teased me about my American boyfriend.

Mike put constant pressure on me regarding marriage. He wanted to get married before getting drafted. The problems this caused me were enormous. I told Mike my heart was set on registered nurse training.

I decided it best to break up in 1966 after grade 11. I was emotionally overwhelmed by the breakup.

Later, Mike got rheumatic fever, which damaged his heart, but saved him from the draft. Some of his friends, who I stayed in touch with for a while, were sent to Vietnam.

My whole family was getting stressed. Mom and Dad were fighting more due to a heavy load of work and activities. Gerry was curling and we were both finishing grade 10. He helped Dad with the cattle and the irrigation. My younger brother seemed depressed.

I cried a lot, felt depressed or sad, and had trouble keeping up. Many couples asked me to babysit, which meant late nights and less sleep.

My 1965 diary indicates a life very much out of control, no boundaries, and an excess of social life. My emotions were out of control. I was having sleep deprivation.

By summer I felt much better, happier, laughing and having fun. By late August I was diagnosed hyperthyroid. A specialist in Kelowna started me on propylthiouracil, an antithyroid medication.

The endocrine specialist explained that I had to stay home from school for a minimum of a month. I had just started grade 11 the week before at Oliver Senior High School. I ended up missing two months.

My aunt took Laurie and me to Comox for a visit. Then I visited a few friends in Vancouver. Mom and Dad took us to Ainsworth Hot Springs for Labour Day weekend.

I was not to do physical work or exercise. I was allowed to go for a drive or to a show. I had to see the doctor every two weeks and have the BMR test at St. Martins Hospital. It checks the basal metabolic rate as you breathe into a machine. In 1965, the accuracy of thyroid tests was limited.

I tried to keep up at home, but it was not easy. My friend Linda brought my homework for me. Mrs. Norcross came to help with my French.

Gradually I became more and more brain-dead and lethargic. I gained 30 pounds. I looked puffy all over, as if I was now hypothyroid. It was hard to stay awake when I went back to grade 11. My marks went steadily down. I had to repeat math.

The medication made me have very slow dreams. I could wake up and write everything down. After the medication was discontinued, my mind and body returned to normal slowly.

Ten years later another endocrine specialist did very important tests on my thyroid gland. The radioactive iodine test indicated that my thyroid was normal and always had been!

I had been improperly diagnosed and treated. The specialist felt that I'd had an emotional disorder, which often affects hormonal function.

7. New High School

Grade 11 at my new school, Oliver Senior High, did not go well. I had missed the first two months, quit chemistry right away, and failed math.

I had gained so much weight, making me self-conscious. My relationship with Mike was taking its toll.

That summer I was able to get a full-time job at the Osoyoos Bakery. The owners were Harry and Dag Jones. It was a family run business and exceptional bakery. I worked in the coffee shop part. We served coffee, tea, milkshakes and fresh baking every day. At lunch I made soup and sandwiches. It was a very challenging job especially adding up things for the not so modern till.

I've always had problems doing any kind of math. Even dealing with four-way stops is confusing for me. I'm told these problems result from the early age when I was traumatized.

Grade 12 was another challenge. I was repeating math 11, had to take extra French, and almost failed economics. I enjoyed geography, foods 11 and 12 and childcare. To get into the nurses training, I had to have minimum requirements.

Our classes were the first to go for the miniskirts and long hair. The school tried to impose a dress code. A letter from the chairman of the school board gave strict orders on how short hair must be and the required length in inches for skirts.

We were defiant and protests were held outside. A photo of the protests made the local paper.

Mr. Reid, the principal, had his hands full. Mr. Shannon, the vice principal, was also very stressed. We were all being very bad, and the school was getting a reputation.

We also had the first grade 13 class included that year. It was difficult to mix with so many new students. Some came from Bridesville and Rock Creek.

My friend Lee and I joined the "Future Nurses" at St. Martins Hospital for grade 11 and 12. In grade 12, we applied at different hospitals at the coast.

The summer of 1967 I got my job back at the bakery.

My diary was very important to me. I could express all my feelings without actually confronting anyone.

Many students failed grade 11, so I was grateful I made it.

I was continually busy with my social life, dating, babysitting, Rangers, the horses and writing letters to too many friends.

Just south of the border there was a very busy drive-in theatre. Oroville, Washington also had a theatre on Main Street. In my younger years Osoyoos had the Sunland Theatre on Main Street. Movies were 25 cents.

Our neighbourhood was changing.

Most farms close by were owned by German immigrants. We also knew Ukrainian, Italian and Swiss families.

In 1968, John and Helina Loura bought the Lemke farm. They had three school-age children.

Frank and Alda Helario bought the Besler farm in 1969. They also had three school-age children.

Our new neighbours were Portuguese. The mothers worked very hard in the home, raising the kids, helping in the orchard, and garden. They did not have much time to learn English. The fathers learned English and got along well with the other farmers.

Many Portuguese moved to Osoyoos starting back in the early 1960s. They worked hard and saved money to buy fruit farms. They were good people and kept their farms well looked after.

8. Letting Out the Secret

The stop for the school bus for high school in Oliver was up the hill on the highway.

A friend in my grade got on at the same stop. We sat together if I wasn't doing my homework.

One day I told her about the evil man and what he had done to us children. It was the first time I had ever opened up and mentioned it to anyone.

I realize I had been thinking a lot about what had happened years earlier and had obsessive thoughts. But it wasn't until years later that I really understood them.

Years later, she told me she had felt sick over it since the day I told her. I never talked to anyone again about it until I was 32.

I was about 35 when I finally went to talk to a male mental health worker. At first, I minimalized things. He got the impression that this guy was an exhibitionist, that he was only going around with his pants open. Of course it was more than that.

The counsellor determined that I had post-traumatic stress disorder, even though it wasn't until almost two decades later that a psychiatrist reached the same conclusion.

As I gradually came to terms with what had happened years earlier, I began reaching out to others who had grown up in the neighbourhood at the same time.

In the 1980s and 1990s, I contacted as many people as I could think of that might have been abused by the pedophile. A number of them admitted to being abused and said I was the first person they'd told.

Some had repressed the memories. A few wouldn't admit they knew anything happened, but they weren't convincing. You can tell when all of a sudden their speech is tied in knots and they don't ever want to talk again.

Some of the people I talked to discussed how our play involved sexual games in our pre-teen and early teen years.

It was copycat stuff, inspired by our experience with the pedophile. It would happen in the neighbourhood sawdust bins. We undressed like he used to make us do and we'd poke around with sticks like the old man did with his poker. I believe that children do that to try to come to terms with what happened.

Some of the other children were also profoundly traumatized. I learned of one girl who died in her 20s after suffering from many emotional problems.

Most of the adults in the neighbourhood had no idea any of this was happening. The children kept it secret in fear.

When the pedophile tried to assault one neighbourhood girl, she told her parents. Her father went down with a rifle and threatened to shoot him. Years later when I told my father about it, he said he would have shot him himself if he'd known about it. I believed him.

My father always supported me on this, perhaps as a result of his own experiences being raped as a young boy. My mother did not. She didn't want to make waves and upset the neighbours. She even asked me why I didn't tell her about it when I was four years old.

In May 1996, at age 47, I typed a letter regarding the pedophile, how he affected my life, and about the "treatment" I'd received due to misdiagnoses. I sent the letter to all my former psychiatrists, medical doctors, mental health workers and a few friends.

In the letter, I emphasized that I wasn't psychotic, neurotic, schizophrenic, insane, crazy or manic depressive. Rather, it was trauma from years of sexual abuse, repressed in secrecy until the memories returned. I said in the letter that one day I would tell my story in more detail as a book.

Many lives were turned upside down by this sick pedophile. The experience had a long and lasting impact on me.

9. Young Adulthood Problems

I was accepted for RN (registered nurse) training at the Royal Columbian Hospital in New Westminster. It was a three-year program.

I had worked at the Osoyoos Bakery until classes started February 1, 1968. It was good to have money saved up, as our stipend was only five dollars a month.

The first three months were straight classes. I loved it all except for "nurses' arithmetic," which involved converting doses to metric. As we went through junior and intermediate blocks, classes were more difficult. Shiftwork became draining.

I was doing better in my second year and passed the exams, but there was also mounting stress. Certain things in my training triggered my anxiety. Two of those triggers were male patients and blood.

Doing personal care of male patients, including quadriplegics, was upsetting. Penises were a really big trigger after dealing with the pedophile all my childhood. The combination of penises and blood brought back memories of how the pedophile did things to himself in front of me until he was bleeding.

I don't think I realized at the time how this part of my training was affecting me. All I knew is that I was feeling really uncomfortable in certain situations.

In spite of that, I did well in operating room nursing for three months and was complimented by surgeons about my ability to keep up with them in emergencies.

Back home, I had a steady boyfriend from Oliver. It was a relationship going nowhere due to his alcoholism. I was taking the bus home every weekend to see him. I had more and more sleep deprivation and emotional turmoil. I broke off our relationship, but it didn't end my problems.

Our intermediate exams were done by the spring of 1969. My marks had improved but my behaviour was worse.

I was not sleeping well. A very kind intern came up to see me at the residence. This was the second time in my life to be put on sleeping pills.

To complicate matters, my classmates and I went drinking and out on very late dates. Because we were so unmanageable, new rules had to be made. At 2 a.m. they locked the doors!

The nursing administration grew very concerned about my health. They thought it might be an overactive thyroid again. My thyroid tested normal, so the next step was to send me to a very clever psychiatrist. He encouraged me to talk about my emotional issues. He started me on a low dose antidepressant. I never saw him again due to what followed next.

I was becoming irritated by all the noise in the residence. Some anger was surfacing.

I was scheduled to come home in July 1969 for a tonsillectomy. I didn't have the surgery but did end up in St. Martins Hospital in Oliver. This was the time of the first moon landing and I'd gone several days with little sleep. I was extremely speeded up and staff were unable to control me. The straitjacket with plenty of ice packs, along with injections, did not calm me down.

After a few days in St. Martins, my doctor had my parents take me to the psychiatric facility in Kelowna under much protest on my part.

Back in 1969 it was called the "Little Brown House." It was a very old two-storey house. It was situated next to Kelowna General Hospital.

Dr. Frank McNair ran the facility. He was arrogant and emotionally abusive. He didn't treat me well and liked to discipline with antipsychotic medication.

He started giving me 30 ECTs, electroconvulsive therapy treatments. It took six months to get my memory back after discharge.

The only positive part of my six months incarceration was Occupational Therapy. I learned macramé, teaching friends for years later. I also did "hippie art" and paintings. We learned tile work and ceramics.

My label was schizophrenia, a common "fits everything" diagnosis often used in the 1960s to 1970s. I had my second misdiagnosis of the period from July 1969 to July 1974.

At no time did Dr. McNair ask me about family history, emotional issues, or traumatic childhood memories. He did not research the fact that I had seen a psychiatrist recently in New Westminster.

My classmates in class 71A were so kind. They sent huge cards so they could all sign them. They never gave up hope. The school of nursing did not accept me back.

After discharge I had to go back for appointments with Dr. McNair or the mental health nurse. The long drive made me look for a new doctor in Penticton.

Six months in a psychiatric unit is devastating. I had lost my self-esteem and self-confidence. I felt slow physically and mentally.

I did some volunteer work at the Osoyoos school. The teachers were helpful and encouraging. Because of the medication, I couldn't move or think very fast.

As I was able to reduce my medication, things gradually improved.

10. Life Goes On

I was able to find a full-time job at Little Duffer's Ice Cream Parlour for the summer of 1970. We served hard ice cream, milkshakes and banana splits. It was just off Main Street and very busy.

I worked with another girl from Oliver. We had a great time. The owners dealt with supplies and supervision.

August 23 was my lucky day! A friend phoned to see if I would like to go on a blind date with her and her husband. Pat and Keith owned the Osoyoos Chevron station.

That evening I met Roman Dust, my future husband. He was very tall, slight build with long blonde curly hair. We all went to Oroville to drink and dance. Three places had live bands.

Roman had his car in getting fixed at Keith's garage. His car was a Datsun 2000 sports car, which was unknown to me. I also found out he was towing a small "hippie" camper. He had converted the van himself. He also painted it with huge flowers.

Roman was always on the move. He had come west from Bruno, Saskatchewan. It is a small town east of Saskatoon.

By fall, he was wanting to explore the coast of B.C. Not long after, I found a live-in job in Burnaby, looking after a young boy. Roman found a room to rent close to English Bay.

The next spring, I applied to Okanagan College for the licensed practical nurse (LPN) course. I had to sit in front of a group and be told I had a mental health problem in my past. Therefore I was denied. They suggested I try working as a dental assistant.

I did line up a job with a dentist in Penticton for September. Roman and I rented an apartment within walking distance of my work.

Roman worked for my dad in the orchard. Mom and Dad got a small single-wide mobile home for us to live in when home.

The dentist I worked for was from England. It was a "one-girl" office and very busy. I was one person doing work that today would be handled by multiple staff people.

I assisted, prepared instruments, sterilized them, and answered the phone to make appointments. At the end of our eight-hour day, I had to clean the office and wash the floors.

I also had the job of getting people to pay their bills. Often, we were taking people in for free extractions right off the street.

I didn't know my dentist friend had a problem. He became more stressed and anxious. He started going into this back room more often and closing the door. He became irritable and difficult to please. I didn't catch on, but often wondered why he was using mouthwash so often.

It soon became evident that the back room was where he kept his alcohol and he was drinking at work. He was definitely pretty loaded on the job.

I quit after nine months and planned to try again to get into LPN training.

It was a relief not to have to deal with his changing moods, strange behaviour and unrealistic expectations of me.

11. Dr. Larry Anderson

My new psychiatrist was just out of training and was new to Penticton. He was very quiet at first and didn't offer much help.

I began seeing Dr. Larry Anderson in the fall of 1971. He acted strangely. I felt fear towards him, and my body had similar feelings to those I experienced being abused as a child.

He wanted to do a series of nine appointments with hypnotism. The sessions were scheduled from 7 p.m. to 8 p.m. at his Martin Street office – after his receptionist was gone.

Dr. Anderson claimed the treatment would make my breasts grow. He dangled objects in front of me to try to hypnotize me. I concentrated on refusing to let myself be hypnotized.

At the time, I had been misdiagnosed with schizophrenia, so hypnotizing me to enlarge my breasts seemed very strange.

The whole time I felt pelvic pain, which I learned in counselling can be an indication that you feel sexually threatened.

He tried to be cuddly. One time I felt very cold. He told me to come and sit on his lap so he could keep me warm. I refused. I couldn't wait to get out of that office!

After a few of those sessions, and well before the completion of the "treatment," he gave up on the idea.

Office visits were very stressful. I would ask questions and he would stare at me, unable to answer.

I asked Dr. Anderson why I was labelled schizophrenic when I had no symptoms. No answer! Thank goodness I wasn't on much medication.

I continued to see Dr. Anderson on and off until 1979, whenever I ended up in the psych ward in Penticton. He was head of psychiatry at the time.

He never actually sexually assaulted me, but I later learned he had a number of inappropriate contacts with other female patients. Nor did he discuss mental health issues – he just wanted to know about my boyfriends, and later about Roman.

In the fall of 1979, I learned that I'd been assigned a new psychiatrist and that Dr. Anderson was no longer working at Penticton Regional Hospital, though at some point he returned.

From 1979 to 1999, I was not involved with any psychiatrist. It took those 20 years before I had the courage to report what happened with Dr. Anderson.

I spoke to Dr. Alexander McIntyre in the summer of 1999 about my experiences with Dr. Anderson and the psych ward. He took notes and seemed to accept what I was saying. That got the ball rolling.

Little by little, other women also started coming forward. It took seven years though until Dr. Anderson was finally put behind bars.

In November 1999, I called the Penticton RCMP. I was told that I had to make the first move as I was the victim. My interview was scheduled in Penticton for December 7 at the police detachment. It takes so much courage to blow the whistle on a sex abuser, especially a psychiatrist!

I was so nervous that my first statement to police didn't actually contain the incidents considered to be sexual assault. I spoke only about the sexual exploitation that occurred during office visits. I remained confused about the abuse, which had occurred on the psych ward on three admissions. Somehow, at the beginning, I thought that they didn't count.

Investigating a doctor takes enormous amounts of time and taxpayers' money. It was worth every penny to get this guy out of circulation permanently.

When Dr. Anderson finally came to trial in 2005, Dr. McIntyre asked me questions and told me he didn't want me on the witness stand. He was afraid of what the stress of testifying would do to me. When they put you on the stand, there's nothing left of you after they pick you apart.

In the end, a jury found Dr. Anderson guilty of two counts of sexual assault and one of indecent assault involving three women – even though there were others who didn't testify. The assaults occurred between the 1970s and 1990s in both Penticton and Vernon.

Crown prosecutor Brent Bagnall acknowledged that none of the women were physically forced to have sex with Dr. Anderson, but because of the doctor-patient relationship and the vulnerability of these women, it was sexual assault, nonetheless.

Dr. Anderson admitted to having sex with the three women but tried to argue it was consensual. The assaults often occurred in his office after staff had gone for the day.

One victim testified that she dropped into his office to pick up a prescription for anti-depressant medication. Instead, Dr. Anderson gave her a note that said: "Take one erection and put it in an appropriate space. Do what is needed to obtain satisfaction."

It must have been very difficult for the three women who testified. Not only did they appear at the trial, but they also had to testify at the preliminary hearing in 2004.

I attended court twice to watch – once when two of the women were testifying and again when Dr. Anderson was sentenced.

In January 2006, he was sentenced to 18 months in jail, but of course he was released much sooner. He also was given two years' probation and was added to the sexual offender registry.

He resigned from the B.C. College of Physicians and Surgeons in 2002 after being disciplined for unprofessional conduct and prior to being criminally charged. In his sentencing, he was also prohibited from seeking reinstatement into the College.

Supreme Court Justice Austin Cullen said Dr. Anderson's conduct was a serious breach of trust over a long period of time. It did damage to the women involved, he acknowledged.

Considering the lives he impacted, he got off pretty easy.

12. Hawaii

With help from my former school principal, I was accepted into the LPN class at Okanagan College. I started in September 1972 and graduated in June 1973.

As soon as the apple crop was done, Roman joined me in Kelowna. We were able to rent at Casa Loma Resort. Roman worked at several jobs in Kelowna.

My RN training started to come back to me, especially the medical terminology. I found things much easier than my classmates.

I took classes seriously and always did my homework. Exams and lack of sleep sometimes stressed me out. I was on a mild sedative after my Grandpa Jim died.

Because of previous RN training I was allowed to take the final month off.

On graduation day I was awarded the highest academic standing, with an average of 95 percent. Everyone was proud of my achievement.

I was accepted to work as a casual LPN at the new South Okanagan Hospital in Oliver. The hospital often called on very short notice. It was a mad rush to eat, dress and drive to Oliver.

I found it hard to stay calm at work. Most shifts were hectic with the work overload. I had anxiety and anger at times.

By late fall, Roman thought we could go somewhere for the winter. We decided to fly to Hawaii with no set agenda.

Air Club International offered return flights to Hawaii for $200. We had to first take a bus to Seattle. The planes were old Boeing 707s.

After drinks and a nice dinner, we had an hour and a half of turbulence. Just about every passenger got sick. It was scary with people screaming and luggage falling from the open racks. For a while, we all feared crashing into the ocean.

Bonnie graduates from her nursing program at Okanagan College in Kelowna in June 1973 to become an LPN.

A taxi bus took us into the Waikiki area. We found a motel for $10 a night, located next to Fort DeRussy.

In a few days, we looked for a cheaper accommodation. Roman found the Driftwood Hotel for $47.50 a week. It turned out to be dirty and have plenty of cockroaches. We cleaned up our room and went for groceries.

We were looking for opportunities in the Honolulu paper. I called a Mrs. Lowe on the north shore and arranged to come out to see her the next morning. The advertisement was for live-in domestic help. We were given instructions on how to find Kuhuku.

We took the bus to the north shore of Oahu and got off at Kuhuku. It used to be a sugarcane mill town.

We walked over to Lowe Inc. and Babs Lowe took us for a tour of the town. We then got to see their property. It was a 15,000-acre lease of land formerly a sugarcane plantation. Now they were growing Sudax (sorghum-sudangrass), similar to corn, for cattle feed.

There was a two-bedroom cottage for help to live in. The older plantation home was five bedrooms and four baths. It had a huge lanai, or veranda.

My job would be housekeeper and Roman would be able to do maintenance and yard work. We anxiously awaited a reply.

On our sixth day on Oahu, Babs called! They would take us on and see how things worked out. Babs came in to pick up our luggage and we took the bus out the next morning. I first had to rush around buying Christmas gifts for my family back in Osoyoos. The Ala Moana was a very small shopping mall back then.

"Babs" was Barbara Lowe's nickname. Art was her husband. Stephen and Kristin were their children.

We took the cottage as payment for the work. Things started to get complicated as time went on. Babs had to spend more time at the office. Art started getting mixed up with some rough characters. I ended up having to babysit as well as do all the housework. Roman helped me out and the kids loved him.

Roman and I either rode the bus, hitchhiked or Babs loaned us her car. We then found a Ford station wagon for $100. It was a 1964 Falcon. Roman did repairs, sanding and painted it blue.

Kuhuku had a regular theatre. It was only 90 cents, so we went often. We had tennis courts within walking distance. We even joined a small typing class.

I sent many letters home. In return, friends wrote about coming to Hawaii. We would plan an outing, pick them up, and give them a tour of part of Oahu.

Three days before my birthday, my dad phoned to see if we could pick him up at the airport! He came over to visit us for two weeks. Dad loved golf and brought his clubs along. Golf was only 50 cents, along the beautiful beachfront of Kuhuku. Dad loved it in Hawaii.

We went to the Kuilima Resort for my birthday. It was the only hotel on the North Shore. It later became the Turtle Bay Hilton.

Dad had good timing as his friends from Regina and Vancouver Island were also on Oahu. Our friends, Pat and Keith, came over and we had outings with them. We kept very busy working and enjoying our vacation.

Later on in February we decided to go camping to another part of the island. We found the Makaha Towers development. Dad wanted us to look for a place he could rent next winter. It looked like a great place. Makaha was very small with mountains and plenty of sandy beaches. Dad did rent at the Towers the following winter, and many more to follow. Two golf courses and plenty of places to walk kept Dad in shape.

We decided to camp at the beach in Maili. A very friendly Hawaiian fellow was fishing nearby. Dale Downey and Roman had identical birthdays.

Dale was worried about us camping but ended up wanting to drink beer and party till 11 p.m. The next morning he brought us coffee. That was our one and only camping experience.

By early March, we decided to move into Honolulu and share an apartment. We drove around to visit the Punch Bowl, National Cemetery, Diamond Head, and the zoo. We discovered Tantalus Drive, which winds up high overlooking Honolulu. The vegetation was thick and hanging over the narrow road.

Peter in our apartment decided to buy our car for $150 when we made plans to return home.

I had some health issues, so it was good to get back in Osoyoos. Hawaii was an unforgettable experience.

This trip was just the first of several to Hawaii.

In January 1975 we were able to visit Dad at Makaha Towers in Hawaii. This time we could be tourists and enjoy our holiday.

Besides the two golf clubs, there were tennis courts and a large pool. I preferred going to the ocean to hunt for shells. It was one of the best areas on Oahu for shells. The reef was dangerous and the surf too rough for swimming. Puka shells were in demand at the time.

Dad had a car on loan with his apartment, so we took many tours all over Oahu. We took photos of locals harvesting pineapples, banana and papaya orchards.

Roman and Dad played tennis or golf often. Dad's main hobby during winters in Hawaii was collecting stray golf balls.

We visited Babs Lowe in Kuhuku. Art was starting shrimp beds along low land next to the ocean. The Sudax idea was not a total success. Eventually Babs and Art split up. Babs and daughter Kristin had moved into Honolulu.

When my daughter was born in 1977, I named her Kristin after the girl I babysat in Kuhuku, Hawaii. Two years later, the two Kristins met.

In January 1979, Roman, Kristin and I went to visit my dad in Makaha. After a week, Roman had to return home as a main water line had frozen.

Dad was able to take Kristin and me into Honolulu to visit Babs Lowe and her daughter Kristin.

13. More Health Problems ... and a Wedding

When I got home from Hawaii, I was bleeding an extreme amount every month. I went to see the thyroid specialist I'd been to in high school. He basically said I had nothing wrong.

My local MD did not believe how much I was bleeding. I had an intrauterine device (IUD) in place called a Dalcon Shield. They were taken off the market due to high risk factors. No one informed me from the gynecologist office in Kelowna.

In Hawaii, I had a positive pregnancy test, and by the time I got home it was negative and I was bleeding. My local doctor had told me not to be a bother.

I then went to a new doctor at the clinic and asked if he would remove the IUD. It would not come out, so he said I'd have to have surgery in Oliver. My own doctor did the surgery. He explained the IUD had grown into my cervix, causing severe pain and bleeding. I'd also had a miscarriage and that explained the upset hormones for three months.

I was trying to work shift work again at the Oliver Hospital. Staff were concerned regarding my behaviour and emotional state. A younger RN was asked to drive me to emergency in Penticton.

My pulse was 140. I was freezing, hungry and thirsty. I was checked over by an internist, heart specialist and MD on call. I was in emergency for six hours; my heart rate was not slowing down. They were not sure what to do. Then they saw Dr. Anderson's name on my chart. They said they would send me to the psych ward. My fears escalated.

In hindsight, if an electrocardiogram (ECG) had been done in emergency, my heart problem would've been diagnosed. I wasn't a psychiatric case. I had started my first episode of paroxysmal supraventricular tachycardia (SVT). It is an electrical problem I was born with. I have had seven episodes since then.

I was on bed rest until my heart slowed. Dr. Anderson had to make a drastic change to my diagnosis of schizophrenia.

My new diagnosis was "manic-depressive," now known as bipolar disorder. It is a mood or affective disorder. I was not given any information to explain my illness.

Dr. Anderson started me on Lithium, a new drug for bipolar. The high dose at the beginning makes you very sick and shaky. I was also on chlorpromazine, a potent antipsychotic.

The psych ward in 1974 was a regular ward on the main floor. There were no locked doors. I hated the smoke-filled patient's lounge and loud TV going all day. I escaped a few times and punishment was an injection or being put in the "lockup" room.

How does one comprehend being labelled schizophrenic for five years then labelled bipolar? I didn't function on therapeutic doses of any medications.

My mother was very concerned regarding my emotions going up and down with my relationship with Roman. We decided immediately and planned a wedding for two days later!

We had a very simple courthouse ceremony in Oliver. I found a $13 wedding dress at Phylis Fashions in Osoyoos. Roman had faded denim jeans and a blue cotton shirt. I bought a $50 ring in Oliver. We had everything then to get married.

That evening we had dinner at Chalet Swiss. Mom and Dad plus my older brother and his wife attended. Mom found a lady to make a wedding cake. I had a pink carnation corsage.

That night we went to Oroville where friends joined us in our celebration. It was a great way to end our wedding day with a live band and dancing.

Roman and Bonnie celebrate their 10th wedding anniversary in 1984. This photo was taken by daughter Kristin when she was just seven.

14. Saving Ceri's Life

I saved a little girl's life back on May 17, 1975. My husband and I had gone camping at the Riverside State Park in Spokane, Washington.

We had a site next to the swift flowing Spokane River. Much debris was floating in the spring runoff. I sat on top of our picnic table, hemming a pair of jeans.

I was watching the river for a minute, when suddenly I saw what appeared to be two small hands. I screamed to Roman as I ran towards the river, discarding my watch and shoes.

I went crashing into the river in an attempt to grab onto the drowning child. The body was being carried away from me into deeper waters. By then an uncle of the child had heard my screams. He was able to dive in, reaching her just in time. I didn't realize at the time, but large waterfalls were just downstream a short distance.

The uncle passed the limp child to me. I was able to get back to shore and carry her up the bank. She was blue and still. I held her up by her feet and whacked her hard across the back, then I laid her down on a slope so the water would drain out of her lungs.

I then did mouth-to-mouth resuscitation as best I could under the stress of the moment. She started breathing! God was with me that day. Her colour started to return and we wrapped her up in blankets. Everyone was pretty much in shock.

Ceri was only two years old. Her parents had just come from England and the aunt and uncle from B.C. They were sharing a tent trailer two sites down. The adults had been busy getting set up and never noticed Ceri slip away.

I went to check on Ceri after getting dry clothes on. Her pupils reacted normally, her colour was good and she seemed to be settling well.

For years I worried about Ceri. I never heard from the parents. I eventually contacted the uncle and got her parents' address. I received a nice letter back confirming Ceri's good health and that she was doing well in school. They thanked me for my bravery and wished me well.

I did not realize I would have flashbacks of the near drowning for years. Ceri's father encouraged me to write a story about it all to help me deal with my emotions.

For years I would recall the whole scene from beginning to end. I worried about the girl, afraid that I might have done something wrong, for example telling the parents they didn't need to take their daughter to emergency because she was recovering.

I think about the danger of what I did. The Spokane River was flowing very high and very fast. I didn't know the waterfalls were just a short distance away. If things had gotten out of control, Ceri would have gone over the falls and I would probably have drowned too because I'm not a strong enough swimmer to fight the currents.

I still get emotional writing about this traumatic event. It was something good I had done in my life, something I could be proud of. For a while it elevated my self-esteem.

15. Motherhood

In August 1975, we took another exciting trip to the Yukon. First, we attended a Dust family reunion in Saskatchewan. We visited Roman's parents before heading north.

The Alaska Highway wasn't paved back then. Most campgrounds shown on the maps did not actually exist. We would end up camping in small towns along the way.

Liard Hot Springs was an awesome place, and very soothing after long days on a rough road.

Our destination was Whitehorse. Roman's friend Arden, and girlfriend Chris, worked there. Arden worked for Trans-North Turbo Airlines.

We had a helicopter tour of the Yukon River and Whitehorse area. We also got to see the Frantic Follies. Side trips included Atlin, B.C. and Haines, Alaska.

It was a very long, dusty trip with next to no traffic.

Coming home we took the Stewart-Cassiar Highway and visited Hyder, Alaska.

On return home I got a full-time job with home support.

On Labour Day 1976, Kristin Lee Dust was conceived at Hart's Pass. We were 6,000 feet up in the Cascade mountains, west of Winthrop, Washington. We like to camp and hike in the beautiful Pasayten Wilderness.

I had to go to emergency when we got home, with severe pelvic pain. It was thought to be an ovarian cyst. I missed my period that month and guessed I was pregnant.

My MD did not believe me. In fact he looked at my bikini incision from my appendectomy and said, "are you sure they didn't take out your ovaries?"

He was judging me by my label on my chart, "manic-depressive." He told me not to come back for the pregnancy test for another six weeks.

I had no prenatal support from my MD. When I developed phlebitis in my right leg, the only concerned person was his nurse, Joan. She knew more about pregnancy and delivery than this doctor would learn in his lifetime.

I had a great pregnancy, ate healthy foods and kept active. Dr. Anderson took me off Lithium before I wanted to get pregnant. I worked full-time for home support until I was seven months.

My only big stress was doing most of the phoning and organizing for our 10-year grad reunion on July 30, 1977.

At the start, I was 113 pounds and did not gain more than the 22 pounds recommended. My doctor presumed I was having a small baby. Little did he know!

I was due May 31, 1977 but ended up with a problem at seven months. The baby got stuck as it tried to turn and lie in a different position. I was only in hospital for a day.

On my due date, my doctor ordered pelvimetry x-rays to check measurements of my pelvis. I had started contractions off and on for three days, and then they ceased. It was not made known to me, until after the fact, that I was heading for a difficult delivery.

On June 3, Roman and I went to the tent sale at Ben Prince's in Oroville. We shopped that evening and stopped at a garage so I could go to the washroom. The cervical plug had come out, and I was starting to bleed. We came home briefly, then went off to the Oliver Hospital.

The chaos was gradual at first. I had asked to allow my husband to be present for the delivery. I had also requested a "rooming-in" for my baby. My doctor was in a very bad mood for the next two days. His weekend off and golf was constantly disrupted.

Roman was sent home for the night and called early the next morning. He was by my side coaching me as I swore in French, counted and did my breathing.

My room and the delivery room started to look like a disaster zone. On the second attempt in the delivery room, my doctor lost his cool.

He said to the nurses, "Don't call me again till the head is coming through!" I was getting more stressed as the day progressed. Finally Kristin presented herself proudly at 4:20 p.m., 8 pounds, 5 ounces, Irish red hair and smiling.

We were having a heat wave while I was in the hospital and the air conditioner there quit working. My room was 80° F (27° C) and Kristin was kept in the nursery at night to help her heat rash. I was breast feeding and dealing with exhaustion. I didn't get much sleep and became overwhelmed by visitors. All the staff knew me, so they were anxious to see my baby.

Four days later I got to go home to our newly air-conditioned double wide. About two days later, my emotions, hormones and stress started to take its toll. My body felt like it was doing strange things. I tried to call my doctor, the one who couldn't be bothered with the delivery, but he was no longer in practice. I was speeding up from lack of sleep. My husband and mother's reactions traumatized me even further. My fear, anger and anxiety escalated.

I asked Roman to take me to the emergency in Oliver when Kristin was eight days old. The doctor on call attended to my problems. I told him I was extremely thirsty and had hormone problems. He immediately diagnosed me as "insane." He said, "I am going to give you a needle to put you to sleep for two or three days and take your baby away from you." I replied, "You are not touching me or my baby. I want to see Dr. Anderson in Penticton."

The comments, lies, and actions of this doctor were atrocious. He went into a back room with my husband to make a phone call to Penticton. They both came back out and the doctor said he had spoken to Dr. Anderson who would meet me at the psych ward. As it turned out, Dr. Anderson was out of Penticton. It was over a year since I had seen Dr. Anderson as a patient.

When I got to the psych ward, things went from bad to worse. The staff put me in a room with orderlies, psych nurses and my husband. They interrogated me for several hours. I became very angry and feared what they were going to do to me. I pleaded with Roman to take me home. He was so afraid and confused. I didn't know what I'd done to indicate I was mentally ill. I had a healthy pregnancy, a stressful delivery and a beautiful baby girl. I knew my hormones were out of whack, which is normal.

I was admitted by nursing staff, hot, sweating and needing to breast-feed my baby. Mary, a very kind nurse, took me to a private room. I was able to shower, change into a gown and feed my baby. The following day I was transferred to the maternity ward.

I felt safe in the four-bed room on maternity until Dr. Anderson came in late that night. His presence made me fearful. He was too close for comfort. I did not trust him touching me. I told the nurses not to let him into my room again.

In a few days, I was sent back to the psych ward. They decided to take Kristin away from me. Medications made breast feeding no longer an option. It took a lot of injections to calm my rage. I think any new mother would've reacted the same.

I got to go home in a month. Fortunately my sister-in-law was able to take time off her job and care for Kristin. After I was home for a week, I was allowed to bring home my baby.

Being a new mom, on enough Lithium to make me vomit and shake, was not easy. I had mental fog from the Chlorpromazine. I was encouraged to see a new medical doctor. I got the much-needed support for my baby and me. He gave me something to counteract the side effects of the Lithium.

Things improved as I was able to reduce my medications.

This started to become a pattern. I'd be really "sick" while in the hospital and improved to normal as I lowered the doses of Lithium and Chlorpromazine. On admissions, I only remember my escalating anger. My follow-up visits to Dr. Anderson were useless.

I explained to my new MD that I never wanted to see Dr. Anderson again. I also expressed my fear of the psych ward. He reassured me he would do his best to keep me out of there. I was safe for two years.

Our 10th grad reunion went over well at the Starlite Motel. We had a dinner and dance on the Saturday night, and a picnic on Sunday at the Osoyoos Lake State Park in Oroville. My classmates took turns holding Kristin.

I tried to forget what happened last June. Deep down inside me, I was still fearful and angry. Without my memories, I did not know what I was afraid of. The medications dulled my senses and feelings.

I became a very busy mom. I enjoyed Kristin so much. I sewed a lot of her clothes, used cloth diapers, and made my own baby food. I was about as "normal" as you could get. My only health issues were deep vein problems in both legs and chronic neck pain from trauma, tension and muscle spasm.

16. Back at the Psych Ward

In September 1978, I was asked to be a Girl Guide leader. Sharon was the captain and I was the lieutenant. It was very bad timing as Kristin was only 15 months old. It was much more than weekly meetings. There were district meetings, parents' meetings, Guider training days and much prep work to do.

The leader lived out of town and sometimes couldn't make meetings, so I had to lead. I was getting stuck with more than I had planned on. At the same time, I was starting to work again as a nurse.

In spring of 1979, work at home, caring for a young child, and my commitment to Girl Guides got the best of me. I had let my doctor know that I wasn't sleeping well. I was irritable a lot.

Our big Girl Guide camp was at Sugar Lake, north of Vernon, the May long weekend. Things were hectic, busy and noisy. By the third day I'd really lost my cool. The stress made me angry. I didn't sleep well and became very exhausted.

When I got home from camp, I was also angry regarding issues and events that happened over the weekend. I went to my doctor again, worried about not sleeping, and maybe "high."

I quit Girl Guides immediately. I went back to my doctor and insisted I needed to be admitted to the Oliver hospital. He was trying his best to keep me out of the Penticton psych ward.

I was admitted at 3 p.m. into a private room. I was freezing, starving and very speeded up. I had my two photo albums of Kristin and her baby book with me. I called home for my big quilt and food. The diet kitchen also brought food and water. To try and warm up I took several hot showers. I had not been given any sedative as yet to calm me down. My doctor dropped by to see me about 5 p.m.

After supper, I managed to get dressed and escape out the exit doors of the south wing. I ran as hard as I could towards the arena. I went to a house to ask to use the phone. It turned out the lady knew me. Her son and I graduated together. I then told her my car had broken down, and I needed to call a taxi.

I had a taxi take me to my friend Pat's, just north of Oliver. I felt safe. I took another hot shower and Pat made up the pull-out couch for me to sleep on. I called my lawyer to explain that I needed protection.

Somehow the RCMP found out where I was (taxi driver probably) then my husband was informed. I did not trust anyone at that point. I feared the psych ward and Dr. Anderson. Two years ago, they had been very abusive in their treatment of me. The male head nurse enjoyed causing physical and emotional pain.

After calming down at Pat's, I agreed to go to the psych ward the next morning at 10 a.m. I had been convinced that I was "manic." I was medicated and never got out for five weeks. Things did not go well. Many other specialists got involved with my case. They also brought in another psychiatrist.

I was given several shock treatments before slowing down. I believe the first three weeks of medication had no effect on me.

I made several escapes from the ward. Back then the doors were un-locked. They'd get the RCMP to track me down. The male head nurse was just as mean and abusive. I was bruised all over from his brutal strength. They sent the "men in the white coats" to hold me down for injections. Four big orderlies and one little lady! My backside was pur-ple from the forced injections, plus a bit of nerve damage.

One day I finally said to them, "Leave me alone, get off me. Just one person give me the injection!"

I was sent home on too much Lithium and Chlorpromazine. I was shaking, vomiting and felt brain-dead.

I missed out on Kristin's second birthday. Roman's mother, Clara, came out to look after Kristin for Roman. Clara had Kristin all potty trained by the time I got home. Things were back to normal in a very short time. Several weeks later, Roman, Kristin and I went camping at Hart's Pass. After that I was busy with friends, canning and making pickles.

By December 1979, I went back to work as an LPN at extended care in Oliver. After a few years, I did private home jobs instead. It was much more enjoyable.

My doctor in Oliver was a great help. I never went back to a psychiatrist for 20 years. I was on a low dose of lithium for the next 14 years. Chlorpromazine was a horrible drug to be on and my physical and mental state improved when it was discontinued.

It took years to sort out my feelings of guilt and shame. A few of the staff on psych encouraged me to take legal action against the hospital. I was not prepared to do that. I had so many unanswered questions.

17. Finding Normalcy

The 1980s were very busy years for my husband and me. There were new trees to plant in the orchard, gardening and yard work. I was growing hundreds of evergreens from seedlings.

We travelled into Washington, Oregon and Disneyland. Later another trip to Sacramento. Sometimes we just went camping to Manning Park or Hart's Pass. I went to Hawaii three times to visit Dad.

April 1988 is the year I braved a trip to England to visit my penpal.

Back home, I helped with thinning and picking when available. When my daughter was older, she was a big help.

I was working as an LPN at extended care after Kristin turned two. Later I did home care jobs in Osoyoos. It was not easy to say no when people asked for help. Things got very stressful at times.

I was only 40 when menopause arrived. It helped explain temperature problems, and drastic mood changes. Stress from work produced tension and years of neck pain.

Some other mothers and I started switching kids so that our children had playmates a few times a week. It worked very well for everyone. Kristin went to ballet, play school and some acrobatics before kindergarten.

I started a monthly craft group. We took turns hosting the evening and teaching a craft. I had the idea from a friend in Vancouver. We made all kinds of fun things and some artistically challenging. I enjoyed learning new crafts and sewing projects.

In the spring of 1990, we moved into our cabin. We had spent two years designing our new home. Our double wide was moved to a site in Oliver. Roman landscaped all around it before selling it. We both worked on the house along with two carpenters. By December we moved in. It was a very exciting time in our lives.

My emotions started to be more labile. I'd be irritable, angry or crying. If I couldn't handle my shift work, I would book off time. My sleep problems started in childhood with nightmares. Gradually flashbacks and nightmares returned. Some of the dreams were about what they did to me on the psych ward.

I was usually only on 300 mg of Lithium, but it slowly made me hypothyroid. It is a common effect of Lithium. In 1993, my gynecologist advised me to quit Lithium because of its effect on my hormones and thyroid. I went the next six years off Lithium.

For grade 11, Kristin and I took a holiday to Seaside on the Oregon coast. It was a fun trip. In grade 12 at Christmas we went to Hawaii. Kristin could not remember all the times she went to see her grandpa.

My years of pelvic pain were finally diagnosed after finding a new female MD. This was after a previous incorrect diagnosis of irritable bowel. When I had a hysterectomy, my problem could not be seen. A CAT scan (computerized axial tomography) determined I had ovarian varicose veins in a large clump, sitting on spinal nerves. A gynecologist arranged for treatment at UBC Hospital. The procedure was called a venogram and embolization. In six months, I was back to normal with no pain, and able to sit and walk around without a problem.

18. Coming to Terms

On April 2, 1995, I decided to walk off some stress along the lake. I'm usually looking for driftwood. I spotted something unusual and as I got closer, I realized it was a dead body. It was a male, face down wearing a shirt, pants and runners. The lake was still partially covered with ice. I ran as fast as I could up the very steep bank and phoned the RCMP. They came, and I had to take them down to the body.

The RCMP subsequently identified the man as a 46-year-old Salvadorian living in Oliver. Foul play was not suspected, and the case was being treated as a "sudden death," according to an article in the *Osoyoos Times.* I can still picture what he looked like, lying with his face down in the water.

This episode continued to haunt me and was an example of how very stressful events affect me for a long time. I've had so many major stressors and triggers all through my life.

On Mother's Day, that same year, I was physically assaulted by a very tough drug dealing lady. She was in a rental house nearby. There were three court dates in Oliver as she had one no-show and one where her lawyer had quit. Charges were successful on third try.

In 1996, my husband read an ad for "Stop the Violence" program. He encouraged me to phone and find out more. They did counselling for adult women survivors of childhood sexual abuse. I was in desperate need of some help, so signed up for the 10 sessions. I suppose the largest benefit was having a safe place to unload all the terrible memories of my past.

It was May of this year I'd had a very clear dream. I dreamt about writing this book. People were allowing me to tell my story for the first time. Back when I had the dream, I typed an information letter. I sent it to important people in my life. I got support from most people, but not my mother, brothers or sister-in-law. My father always supported me because of his own abuse issues. I even got a few threats to keep my mouth shut. I had validation by 10 other children abused by the same pedophile.

The daughter of the pedophile had the power to control the secret. I became the scapegoat while other adults kept quiet.

By 1997 I was able to do a very long typed confrontation presentation for the neighbour. My lawyer checked it out for me first. There was no denial this time. It took so much courage to do this. It's part of the recovery process to do a confrontation.

Through all this commotion, our daughter Kristin managed to graduate with honours and many awards. She worked hard all through school and her summer jobs. She went on for 10 years at three universities. Her final goal was a master's in environmental economics.

The year 1997 was exciting. I had my last trip to Hawaii for two weeks. My friend Thelma was already staying at Waikiki and I was invited to join her. The highlight was climbing Diamond Head. I took a sketchbook for my trip instead of a camera.

On the long August weekend we had our 30th grand reunion.

On August 26, a freak mini tornado touched down in parts of Osoyoos. It hit the west side of our house, taking out three of our largest evergreens. We also had 12 big red delicious trees flattened. It was a combination of heavy rain and wind. It continued up the valley.

My last full year before being shoved back into a box and labelled bipolar once again was 1998. For 20 years I managed without a psychiatrist or all the medication used for your average bipolar person.

19: The Return of the Bipolar Diagnosis

In 1999, I was first referred to an endocrine specialist in Kelowna. He told me I wouldn't get well until the old shed of the pedophile was gone. It was so dilapidated, an eyesore and constantly in my face when I went out walking.

My weight had dropped to 102 pounds and my sleep problems and anger increased. I was on Paxil then Zoloft, both antidepressants. I was having private counselling sessions.

In May, I did a solo camping trip in our van for nine days. I was in Enderby, Salmon Arm and Princeton. In Salmon Arm, I looked up an old girlfriend who used to be a neighbour. She had known the pedophile and his habits. To talk with her was a definite trigger. By May 30, I was in emergency getting Xanax, a benzodiazepine for anxiety and panic disorder, one more prescription.

My female regular doctor found no psychologist for me to talk to in the Okanagan. She lined up a new psychiatrist for me to see June 3. I was scared and in full-blown panic attack as I gave him details on Dr. Anderson. I also told him about the physical and mental abuse I endured on the psych ward. He was very respectful and noted all my information. Zoloft and Xanax were discontinued "cold turkey," and he started me on Epival and Zopiclone. Epival is used to treat bipolar disorder and epilepsy. Zopiclone is used for insomnia.

My new psychiatrist didn't know about my childhood trauma events or any traumas in care of mental health. I had this one label "bipolar" and it just follows you around. Over the years my problems had more to do with lack of sleep and obsessive thoughts of my past.

I went back to my psychiatrist July 12 and said I'd like to go to a quiet hotel to rest. He said he couldn't afford a fancy hotel, but I could maybe go to Braemore Lodge. I knew nothing about it but went for nine days. It was so hot and no air conditioning. The medications never fizzed on me. My doctor then got me to move over to the psych ward. It was so cool there that I appreciated the move. I was gone from home less than a month. I began therapy again and my doctor switched my sleep medication to Restoril.

In December, I went to the Penticton RCMP to give my statement on Dr. Anderson.

In 2000, I tried to fit in at support groups for bipolar or mental health but didn't have anything in common. I kept busy in the orchard thinning, pruning, gardening and building my grotto.

My "grotto," down by the lake in the northeast corner of our property, became my sanctuary. I began to build it before I thought of the word or its meaning.

In Latin, it is "crypta," a small concealed cave made for coolness or pleasure. There are many meanings and purposes.

I needed a safe, secluded place to call my own. It is where I take my spirit when it needs calming or comforting.

At first, building a "grotto" in the way that I did was seen as odd, abnormal behaviour. Roman was very worried about me spending so much time in the bush. Gathering driftwood, old boards, logs and dead branches is a continual process. My emerging anger became channeled in a positive, creative manner.

My sitting bench is at lake level, completely hidden from the view of passing boaters. Dogwood trails across the driftwood wall and ivy winds in and out the bottom. Taller sandbar willow droops slightly over the wall. Ivy hangs from elm trees all around me.

I welcome friends and family to my grotto to spend a few moments or longer, to enjoy the sounds of nature.

I imagined and planned my "country cottage retreat" at our cabin.

Mark came to rent from me for three months. It turned out to be a very busy summer. Mark, Roman and I all got along well. Mark was so hyper and fun to be with.

I was presuming still that I was bipolar, and Mark presumed he was too. It was a very interesting summer.

After the endocrine specialist in Kelowna told me I wouldn't be well until the pedophile's shed was gone, I confronted the pedophile's daughter and told her what the doctor said. She told me she didn't have to take it down and she didn't want to. It was a heated discussion and I swore at her.

By this time the shed was little more than boards hanging together. I had already spoken to the police and the fire department about getting it removed.

I felt like a hostage with the shed there. I wanted to be able to walk freely on the road without seeing it and all it reminded me about. I was angry about it and the anger was hard to control.

One time I made a voodoo doll and hung it from a noose on the door. Twice I tried unsuccessfully to burn down the shed.

Then one day, two years later, Roman told me he saw the shed being demolished and taken away.

Fifty years of reminders of the abuse ended. I could walk again without freaking out. No one connected my stress to my childhood, except counsellors. They allowed you to talk about your past abuse.

I did a major trip to the Yukon. Our daughter was at Beaver Creek working for the summer. She said she had to drive home alone, so I said I'd fly up to Whitehorse, and we enjoyed a trip home together.

By fall I started sessions with a very nice doctor who became my first psychologist. It was therapy provided by the RCMP in relation to Dr. Anderson. When dealing with my past, my hormones and emotions were constantly out of balance.

One day in 2001, an old friend was staying in town a few days. We got together but things did not go well. My friend talked so excessively, especially regarding religion, that I had to make an emergency trip to my psychiatrist. My doctor started me on Lithium along with Epival and Restoril.

My mom went to outpatients for surgery in Penticton. It was only supposed to be a cyst under her chin. The surgeon phoned to tell me they also discovered a large vascular tumor. He said he was able to get a vascular surgeon on call, and continue the surgery while Mom remained under anesthesia. In 2004, I had the same tumor and surgery in Kelowna.

My medications failed to impress my doctor or myself. I discontinued Epival then Lithium. My next try was Lamictal, an anticonvulsant medication used for bipolar disorder and epilepsy. My key issues of insomnia, anxiety and ongoing stress were not ever dealt with.

In April, Kristin and I drove out to visit Grandma Dust in Saskatchewan. On the way back, we went to Cypress Hills through Montana, Idaho and up to Creston. I was on the bus to Victoria for Kristin's birthday in June.

20: New Doctor and PTSD Diagnosis

On January 16, 2002, I agreed to go to the psych ward to reassess my medications. Two days later I gave my psychiatrist a long letter giving details of my abuse in 1977 and 1979 at Penticton Hospital. I was transferred to Kelowna so that I would be in a "safe" place for reevaluation and second opinion.

I had requested this review as a result of new information about post-traumatic stress disorder (PTSD) that I had been studying for several years.

I needed to prove that I was not bipolar but had PTSD. To be your own advocate is very powerful! To take charge of your own life and resolve a lifetime of health issues is the ultimate reward for this effort.

I was started on Epival again, Seroquel, Restoril and Clonazepam. I only stayed four nights in Kelowna and eight in Braemore Lodge in Penticton.

Epival is used to treat epilepsy and bipolar disorder. Restoril is used to treat insomnia and Clonazepam is a tranquilizer used to treat seizures and panic disorder. I had been on these before.

Seroquel was new to me. It's an antipsychotic used to treat schizophrenia, bipolar disorder and major depressive disorder.

To start, stop or reduce the dose of Seroquel, you must go slowly. I was started on 25 mg, then gradually worked up to 150 mg total daily over an 11-day period.

At one point I was told to go from 100 mg to 200 mg at bedtime. That proved to be a big mistake. The next morning I discovered I had been sleepwalking and eating. The kitchen was upside down. I don't remember any of it. I went back to my lower dose.

I was told it would help my symptoms of PTSD, would help me sleep and improve my cognitive thinking.

I never needed more than a non-therapeutic amount, which is about 150 mg a day. I could always tell when the dose had to be reduced. Even the 25 mg in the morning was enough to put me to sleep.

I was encouraged to stay on it as it appeared to have benefits, such as nine hours in bed. My night was spent drinking sips of water to relieve the dryness it caused. The dreaming it produced became physically draining. By morning I felt hung over. I gradually kept lowering my dose for the next five years.

Sometimes I went off it completely the way the doctor suggested. I learned that this does not work. By doing research, I found it can take up to six months to reduce Seroquel by 50 mg each time.

I managed to cut the round 25 mg pill in half. That allowed me to succeed finally. Five years later, I was off Seroquel.

The plus side of going off Seroquel includes an increase in lost creativity and return of sociability. It is good to focus on positives rather than the withdrawal symptoms, which included difficulty sleeping, temperature fluctuations and nervousness.

I was fortunate to be in the care of doctors who only gave me a small dose of Seroquel.

Psychiatric drugs can harm or be lethal in the wrong dose to the wrong patient. I've been in a temporary vegetable state many times.

Some factors are not taken into consideration when drugs are hastily prescribed or given. For myself, they need to realize that very minimal doses are required due to extreme sensitivity, being underweight and older. If they combine two or three drugs, they make side effects worse. It is in your best interest to know all the side effects, precautions, drug interactions, etc. With my nursing background, I can read the pharmacy drug book and that is where you find the most critical information.

As a result of the reassessment, my new diagnosis became PTSD (post-traumatic stress disorder).

January 30, I started fresh with a new psychiatrist. He was recommended by my former doctor. My new doctor was highly trained in PTSD. I began to feel confident we were getting to the root of my lifelong problems.

A diagnosis of PTSD requires exposure to an extreme stressor. Many situations can be extreme stressors, including a serious accident, natural disaster or exposure to combat.

Childhood sexual abuse is one such stressor used as an example in the Expert Consensus Treatment Guidelines for Posttraumatic Stress Disorder: A Guide for Patients and Families, which is based on survey responses by 100 experts.

There are three main types of symptoms, according to these guidelines:

- Re-experiencing of the traumatic event;
- Avoidance and emotional numbing;
- Increased arousal.

The re-experiencing can include such symptoms as intrusive distressing recollection of the event, flashbacks, nightmares, and exaggerated emotional and physical reactions to triggers that remind the person of the event.

Patients can avoid activities, places and thoughts related to the trauma and can lose interest and feel detached. Thoughts can also become obsessive.

Increased arousal can include difficulty sleeping, irritability or outbursts of anger, difficulty concentrating, hypervigilance and an exaggerated startle response.

Not only could these symptoms lead to possible misdiagnosis of other mental health problems, but they seemed to fit exactly what I had been experiencing.

I continued with Stop the Violence as needed, and sessions with the psychologist.

The usual stress continued on the farm. Always plenty of work in spring, summer and fall. In March I hired Attila. He worked with me for a number of years, just as I needed him. It was fun and he was a big help in the garden and landscape.

In September, we met up with Kristin and took a short trip to Saturna Island. Volunteers helped in October to plant the lakeshore area to natural habitat. It had been apple trees previously.

Somehow, I hiked Throne Mountain with Roman. I have only done it once. At the time I was not aware of my heart problem, which might have been triggered. We look at Throne Mountain every day, and it's a spectacular view from on top.

December 23, my daughter was to come home, and take me to Penticton for ultrasound on my neck. She ended up with a flat tire, so I went alone. I'd had a lump by my left carotid artery for over a year. The test confirmed that I had a carotid body tumor. The staff indicated to me that they run in families. I told them about my mom.

Well, the whole day was shot. I freaked out and went down to psych. I asked if I could sit and have tea. They gave me an injection of something that paralyzed part of my face. I was put in isolation one night, then off to Vernon psych for three days at Christmas. My psychiatrist in Vernon encouraged me to read The Trauma Workbook.

In preparation for surgery I needed a CAT scan angiogram and another of my head. The surgeon in Kelowna had a serious talk with me regarding the possible outcome of the surgery. The tumor was in the crotch of the carotid artery leading to the brain.

Roman left for California a few days before Kristin came home to take me to Kelowna for surgery.

My lifelong friend Pat, in Kelowna, graciously put up Kristin and me when it was time for surgery. It was a blessing to eliminate some of the stress. The surgery went well, and the carotid body tumor was removed without complications.

My mother had recently moved to town, a dream of hers for many years. My younger brother came home to look after Dad. He wasn't well enough himself to be a caregiver to Dad. I tried to provide hot meals for a while until they got meals delivered. It became a difficult year, especially for Dad.

I went back on Lithium for a while. Back then I don't think anyone realized it helps the irritability and anger symptoms of PTSD. In June a case conference was held in Osoyoos on my behalf. My psychiatrist, psychologist, MD and two mental health workers were present.

Thelma and I made our last trip to Salmon Meadows in June. She was my mentor, an expert on all the wildflowers of BC.

I was always trying out new medications to help insomnia. Trazodone was a possible solution. The side effects created further problems.

Roman and I went camping up to Hat Creek Ranch, Riske Creek, Kleena Kleene and Loon Lake.

I was able to trade in the Tracker Roman picked out for "my" car. I needed an automatic. I now have a Suzuki Grand Vitara. It is the only car that I have ever owned myself. It was four years old when I bought it. It took years to get this far.

December was not a good month. My dear friend Thelma passed away, and I would miss her friendship for many years. A clever and most interesting lady. We used to swim together at Adriatic then go back to her place for tea. One hot summer day she had me swimming in Peanut Pond!

Ten days after the loss of Thelma, my father fell in his kitchen. He broke his hip and put a deep gash in his head. At emergency, they started to plan brain and hip surgery. Dad was 94 years old, very frail and breathing with difficulty. I asked the doctor if they could just give my dad something for the pain. Dad passed away the next day, sleeping peacefully.

21. Hikes and Travels

On May 1, 2005, Roman Kristin and I hiked to McIntyre Bluff north of Oliver. The highlight was a large number of chocolate lilies.

On May 21, a group of us tried to climb Mount Chopaka to the west of Osoyoos. It was too early in the year and the cold prevented us from reaching the very top. Later on, Roman, Kristin and I made it to the top. What an exhilarating feeling.

In August, we hiked up Idaho Peak near New Denver, B.C. The flowers were at their best. I got a few very nice pictures. We talked to a butterfly expert trying to catch a few rare species.

I enjoy hiking along mountain trails lined with many colourful flowers. We try to identify as many as we can. A few nice photos are a reminder of how beautiful these alpine meadows are.

Just before Christmas, we went up the road to Mount Kobau to cross country ski. Mostly working our way up a stretch then out of control coming down.

Roman and I went to the Oregon coast in February 2006 to camp. It was sunny every day, so we really enjoyed the trip. We came back through Vancouver to visit Kristin. She was in a tizzy after meeting Oless, who became our son-in-law two years later.

In May and October, I did my solo camping to Enderby. Our van was too small for two people to camp comfortably. I camped along the river in the municipal campground. It is an easy walk or bike ride into town.

Solo camping is very beneficial to freedom of your soul. It was a chance to be independent and to enjoy my own company.

Kristin graduated in June with a master's in environmental economics from Simon Fraser University. That was a very special day for all of us.

Oless has a father and stepmom in Kamloops. They invited me to come up for Thanksgiving. Roman was on a trip to Saskatchewan. Everything went well until the day I headed home. At Monte Lake, I stopped to take a photo. I went back to my car and it wouldn't start. A fellow helped out by phoning for a tow truck. Well, Joe came in a big old flat deck truck wearing cowboy boots and hat! He was wonderful. He dropped off my car, then took me to the Village Green in Vernon.

In February 2007, I was in court regarding my older brother assaulting me. He and I had been on bad terms for many years, and one day he came at me in a rage as I was just trying to walk down the road.

The judge wanted to hear my story of the pedophile. He did not believe the neighbour, who had lied, hoping to deny anything had gone on. The validation from the judge was overwhelming.

A few days after court, I went up in the mountains to stay three nights at Grouse Ridge bed-and-breakfast near Rock Creek. It was three days of good food, company and walking in the snow.

That trip came about after an argument with Roman. He was worried that I wasn't getting enough sleep and he made a comment about it. I said that seven and a half hours in bed was fine and normal. He was used to me being on Seroquel and in bed for nine hours.

I think he was also concerned over me crying so much watching tear-jerking movies. I felt good being able to cry, laugh and have fun again. He had been programmed for more than 30 years that being emotional meant that "Bonnie" was getting sick again.

I "lost it." I told him I was going away as soon as I was packed. He called my mom and asked her to speak with me.

Rather than trying to dissuade me, she recommended the B&B near Rock Creek, which she'd heard about from a friend.

I packed and dressed for the colder temperatures higher up the mountain. It was best that I arrive around 2 p.m., so I had time to fill my husband in on my plans. Kristin also phoned, worried at first, but then happy that I was going away for a break.

A half hour east of Osoyoos, at the turnoff for Conkle Lake Provincial Park and the B&B, I put my Suzuki in four-wheel drive and slowly followed the road in. This B&B was run by Carol and Wilf Carlton.

On this sojourn, I felt no fear, no sadness or anger. I just felt a freedom to live my life the way I choose.

I stayed three nights. By the third night, I felt very calm, relaxed and back to centre.

Everything about my room felt comfortable, cozy and safe. A window looked out over the snow-covered hills, trees and mountains to the east.

I took long walks with Nook, the family Husky, and then climbed back into bed for an afternoon rest.

I was thoroughly spoiled with gourmet dishes I'd never had before. Wilf loaned me some snowshoes and I made my first attempt at it, getting a very good workout in the deep, slushy snow. The birdfeeders were busy with chickadees, a nuthatch, a hairy woodpecker, flicker, gray jay and Steller's jay.

My walks were in silence except for the snowflakes landing on my hat and maybe a crow or jay in the distance. For three days, I did not see another person or vehicle other than Carol and Wilf. I was grateful for the solitude.

I'd brought along my "adult" butterfly colouring book and actually finished my first page. My creative abilities had been blocked by medication for years.

Spring got busy as usual with landscape, garden, grotto, north barrier, weeding and picking Saskatoon berries. Barb next door helped me do puncture vine along our 89th St.

One day we stopped to say hello to my elderly friend Nina. She had three little cabins on property just north from ours. A male friend of hers was waiting to give her a ride back to Vancouver. We helped weed a patch for Nina, then went to the lake to cool off. I wasn't expecting what happened next. The friend lunged at me twice, grabbing my left breast, then my buttocks. I ran up the steep bank and home, avoiding Nina.

My heart was going very fast. The friend even came up to our house and looked around for me, with Nina waiting in the car. Roman does not like involving the RCMP, so I put it off.

The first thing I did was write Nina's friend a letter. I knew him from a few visits and buying some apples from Roman. I told him never to come near me again.

The incident made me feel unwell the next few days. I had pain up and down my neck, plus difficulty breathing. I soon realized it was my heart, my chest bouncing, my pulse too rapid to count. I was having my first documented SVT or paroxysmal supraventricular tachycardia. Basically it is an electrical problem and is congenital.

I was in emergency at least five hours. My heart was not slowing down, so I was given intravenous medication to stop the heart, then it was restarted with another medication. I had to be admitted for two nights.

August 3 and 4 we celebrated our 40th grad reunion at Nk'Mip Desert Cultural Centre. I think everyone enjoyed themselves. This was our fourth reunion for the class of '67.

Early October I went on an adventure. First, I went to Harrison Hot Springs. I dined and danced then enjoyed the hot pools. I then went to Maple Ridge for seven days, visiting Kristin and Oless.

Oless's parents, Soula and Allan, joined us. Roman came for a few days and brought me a few things for Harrison. I just had to go back and treat myself to some live music and dancing.

Soula and Allan had mentioned a dinner and dance in Kamloops in early November. It would be at the Ukrainian Hall. I decided to go even though I had no idea of how to drive to or within Kamloops.

I stopped to see my psychologist, to give him some apples. I was excited to be on another adventure. Maybe "high," but not manic. I then ended up at mental health, then in a private room in emergency.

Someone had put up the red flag. I was alone in this room, so I decided to run for it. I got outside and circled around the hospital, then walked up to my car at mental health. I was in the flight or fight the moment they took me to Penticton emergency.

I took the Okanagan connector to Merritt, then Coquihalla to Kamloops. Because I was delayed in Penticton, it was dark when I pulled into one of the first motels. I let mental health know I was safe. I told my daughter where I was, not aware that someone would come. She called Roman, who contacted the RCMP. A female constable came the next morning and said I had to go to emergency.

Psych in Kamloops said I was "angry," so I was in a small ward for two nights.

From Kamloops I was taken to Penticton psych for another long incarceration. I was not home for 36 days. Zprexa was the next antipsychotic tried on me, plus Epival and a heavy dose of Clonazepam.

The psych ward can be a very stressful environment when you would prefer quiet and rest. The staff and toilets flushing kept me awake at night. Now that my PTSD psychiatrist had moved away, I was in for many more admissions.

22: In and Out of Psych Wards

On May 31, 2008, Kristin and Oless got married in Kamloops in a large Ukrainian wedding. It was hot, exciting and too much to handle. I was off track again a month later.

I went to Hope to visit one night and checked out a single-wide trailer for sale. I thought it would work out as a place to stay closer to Kristin.

I went on to Harrison Hot Springs for three nights. On the third night, I had a problem being locked out of my room with a key card that didn't work. They let me sleep out by the fireplace.

My husband had called the RCMP because he was concerned about me wanting to buy a trailer. An RCMP officer came and he told the night manager that he couldn't arrest me as I was sleeping.

It seemed that every time I tried to spend a dollar on myself, a red flag went up, as though that was a sign that I wasn't well.

The next morning another RCMP came and took me to emergency in Chilliwack. I wasn't anything but angry. I had a cell phone so I could pretend to phone anyone.

It was my single wide plans that started this whole mess. I had to leave my car and belongings behind, eventually being taken to psych in Penticton. I was in psych June 28 until August 1.

They severely overmedicated me. My skin burned badly and turned dark purple from the large doses of Clonazepam. I had been told to go out and relax in the sun. Impaired by the medication, I also fell on the floor one day, and then accidentally poured boiling water over my hand at the dispenser.

Despite medications and being sent home, I still got into trouble. I decided to buy $25,000 worth of office supplies in Osoyoos. My only excuse is that I love paper and wanted a computer.

Kristin and Oless were married on May 31, 2008.

I went voluntarily to see a former psychiatrist in Penticton, then said I wanted to talk to a lawyer down the street about marital financial control. From there I walked to the RCMP station. I was wearing my "Leave Me Alone" T-shirt Kristin had given me.

A male and female officer took me to emergency via the A&W. I needed a burger and milkshake.

About six nurses pinned me down and stripped off my clothes. One gave me an injection of Haldol. I hadn't even done anything to warrant such abuse. I had simply told them I was drinking my milkshake and had not otherwise resisted. When they told me they were going to give me a Haldol injection and Ativan, I said I would take the Ativan, but not Haldol, an anti-psychotic medication.

Sadly the female officer was present when staff viciously attacked me. She said she was sorry and that she didn't know they would do this to me

When a red flag goes up for someone who they say is a manic person, they round up everybody they can get and just storm the person. This is the way they operate. One nurse seriously injured my shoulder.

Usually in that situation I've got all the same symptoms of fear and I'm shaking, cold and hungry.

I was locked up in the "rubber room," which looks like a prison cell with a toilet. I was bombed on the Haldol and could hardly walk. They gave me some quilts because I was freezing and brought me some food. The next day they took me to Kamloops.

I had frozen shoulder for over a year from the one nurse who felt a strong hold was necessary.

My next plan, to join a tour group and fly to Ecuador after seeing an ad in the paper, caused another major issue. I had never been to Ecuador and it sounded exciting.

The problem is that as soon as you're feeling good, people want to say you're manic. I've been told I was manic because I was dressed nicely for an appointment. They probably considered my desire to go to Ecuador as an indication I was totally high.

I seemed to be at the psych ward more than at home. This time I ended my psych time with a week in Braemore.

These journeys to the psych ward were not helpful. Penticton psych ward was a major trigger for my emotional state.

The psych ward was noisy. The staff would chat and laugh and talk all night. In earlier days, the television blared, and the ward was thick with cigarette smoke. Thankfully, the TV was now in a separate room and all smoking was done outside on the patio.

If the staff was close to you, sleeping was impossible. If there was a violent person on the psych ward, you had to put up with their behaviour.

There was nothing to do and the days passed in boredom.

I didn't regret not seeing anybody. I didn't have very many visitors and I didn't miss that. I think I was probably relieved to have three meals a day.

It was actually a relief that I could just go somewhere and not have to do anything and someone was going to fix my meals. It was a break from the stress at home.

There was no counselling in the psych ward. The doctors were erratic – one time when I was in the psych ward, I had four different psychiatrists.

I don't think the psych wards have improved much over the past 40 or 50 years. It's not like other branches of medicine that have gone through major changes with technology. Psychiatry has been on the back burner all this time.

I don't think I got much out of the psych ward. I was probably more depressed than anything.

Most of the people in the psych ward are depressed and they were on so much medication that they were like zombies. The majority smoke constantly.

I don't watch TV and I find I can't read a book or anything when I'm in a psych ward. I just look forward to the food. I spent much of my time walking if I had suitable clothes and shoes.

* * *

In May 2009, Roman actually went to Harrison with me and enjoyed the dinner and hot pools. We did two nights, then had a visit with Kristin and Oless.

May 29, I was asked to come into the Osoyoos RCMP to give my statement of the incident with Nina's friend. A member of the RCMP was taping me as I read my statement.

Then a female RCMP barged in saying a constable had to take me to emergency in Penticton. Another 24 days on psych!

The RCMP apparently assumed I had mental health issues and never followed up on anything.

July 30, my psychiatrist sent me to Kelowna psych with apparent toxic levels of Epival. This was only for one night, then back to Penticton psych. My doctor put me on Haldol, and I seized up like a statue.

Epival is used to control manic episodes and Haldol is an anti-psychotic. I was always given bipolar medications despite the fact they never helped. Anti-psychotics made things much worse.

Two days later I was sent by ambulance to Hillside Centre in Kamloops. I was there till September 23.

The Haldol was discontinued and replaced with Risperidone. Joey was my therapist/social worker. She seemed to know what I needed. Up until now, no one ever talked to me about my life out of the hospital. Somehow my PTSD diagnosis by three psychiatrists got put on the back burner. At Hillside I had no major problems. I did become emotional in therapy. Joey was great. She said if I hadn't been born and raised where I was exposed to a pedophile, I never would have been sick.

In October I went shopping in a big way for groceries in Oroville and clothes at the thrift shop. My husband, concerned about my spending, raised the red flag and somehow, I was back in psych. After five days, I was transferred back to Hillside for 15 days. I spent most of my days resting and walking. Hillside treated me as if my shopping spree was fairly normal.

By now, these psychiatrists must be starting to realize anti-psychotics are not a solution to my problem. For a bipolar problem, they would be helpful in the acute manic phase. My problem is related to ongoing fear, anger, stress and overproduction of norepinephrine.

The 20 years, 1979 to 1999, I proved I could remain healthy mentally on minimal amount of Lithium and no psychiatrist. Lithium does decrease norepinephrine in the brain. Emotional states are directly related to the brain concentration of norepinephrine. Excess amounts of this hormone produce excited emotional states.

I was preparing myself to inform these doctors that I'd had enough and wanted to go back to Lithium.

Roman left for Arizona January 13, 2010 until March. I had decided to take some files to Interior Savings Credit Union in Oliver. I didn't park properly between the lines. I asked if I could set up an account, only I had forgotten my wallet, so I had no ID. I jokingly said the police next door would know who I was. Apparently my behaviour was seen as abnormal. Two officers came in minutes and one drove me up to Oliver emergency.

Apparently the RCMP and the hospital have me flagged on their computers as being bipolar rather than affected by PTSD. Despite my updated diagnosis, the information about me has never been updated.

The doctor said there was nothing wrong with me, but he'd send me to Penticton. That was my final death sentence.

I got up for meals only and stayed in bed the rest of the time. As a result my left leg filled with blood clots which had to be treated quickly and efficiently. A very kind doctor came to the ward to deal with this issue along with many lab technicians.

I didn't like my psychiatrist on the ward, so asked for a second opinion. A big meeting was held, and I made sure I was included. I told the doctors and staff that I wanted no more crap. I just wanted Lithium. I was started on 300 mg and never more than 600 mg. A therapeutic dose is usually 900 to 1200 mg.

I don't think anyone wanted to see me brought into the psych ward. My entire stay was negative, boring and depressing. There was no therapy. I wanted to be home to look after the garden and landscaping. They wanted me to stay till March 3 then live at Braemore till May 25. At Braemore, I went walking or bike riding every day. Meals are always great at Braemore.

I started getting blister packs which makes it easier to organize medications and not forget to take them. I had to be on Warfarin for blood thinner. It requires so many lab tests and gave me frequent nosebleeds.

Well this was it. My very last admission to psych happened in 2010. The best part is I told them what would work for me.

I continued to see a female psychiatrist in Penticton for a year or more. It wasn't often, but she was very nice. My new psychiatrist treated me like a normal person. I was on minimal medication and given much support.

23. Family Matters

My mother was getting sick often and ended up moving to Mariposa Gardens care home. I helped her whenever possible. At one point my mother was on 15 prescriptions while living alone, with no blister packs even. Very scary!

In late September 2011, we went camping at Kokanee Provincial Park, Kaslo and Lost Ledge. We love it over in that area. I love exploring Nelson and Kaslo shops and restaurants. We're always looking at rocks and driftwood. Camping by the lakes provided much shoreline for our explorations.

On June 8, 2012, Roman's mom turned 100 years old. We flew out for birthday celebrations in Humboldt, Saskatchewan. Clara decided that was enough living and passed away a month after the party.

In September we camped again in our RV up in Vernon, then Nakusp, New Denver, Kaslo and Lost Ledge. The RV makes camping easy, especially meal preparation.

In October we actually went to Harrison for two nights and to see Kristin and Oless a few nights. October 21, it snowed like crazy in Mission. Kristin was due to have her first baby two weeks after coming home for Christmas.

January 18, 2013, Roman and I became proud grandparents to Orysia. Kristin asked me to be there for her six-week C-section recovery. We worked in shifts, taking time for rest breaks. A very special time for everyone.

This year I hired Diane to help when I needed her. She has been a very positive influence in my life. Over the next five years we had fun workdays, and some social times together.

Diane was a good worker, always cheerful, and loved our work in nature. It was great to have a friend to talk and laugh with regularly.

December 20, we had a flood in the basement from the water softener. We had similar floods from hot water tanks. It involved a lot of bending to get things off the floor and carpet. Things had to be put somewhere to dry out. So after two days cleaning up, my heart had an episode and my pulse was 174. No doubt the excessive bending over and climbing stairs triggered my SVT.

They treated it at emergency with the heart stopping intravenous.

December 31, I left on my first trip to Arizona with Roman. February 1, I had to fly back as the insurance company wouldn't cover me, due to my trip to emergency. Arizona was great, but too far to travel for me. I was really impressed with Valley of Fire and it was the only place I got lost in the desert. We could walk, bike or hike every state park we travelled to.

As of January 6, 2014, I was on a new blood thinner Eliquis. No more nosebleeds or INR (international normalized ratio) tests!

I flew home to Bellingham and Kristin rescued me. After a visit, I got the bus back to Osoyoos.

In August, I still wasn't sleeping, so went back on some Seroquel. I fell one night damaging my left eye. The Seroquel can make for risky walking at night.

September 1, I had a terrible wasp attack in my grotto. I was using a rake in dry leaves, accidentally disturbing a nest. I was a mess with about 10 stings on my face and head. In about 24 hours I was back to normal.

We enjoyed another camping trip to Nelson, Riondel, Lost Ledge and Nakusp.

December 28, baby Orrin arrived nine days early. We drove down in the RV so Roman could head south and I would stay and help Kristin.

January 24, 2015, Mom passed away while I was at Kristin's. I could not go home yet as I was needed in my own family. I wouldn't miss all the emotional abuse or "button pushing" by my childhood family.

I had three shorter SVTs spaced out over eight months. They stopped on their own.

24: Moving Forward and Reliving the Past

I went with Roman to Arizona again in 2016 for six weeks. We enjoyed time spent with Bill and Marge, Roman's friends from Colorado. I got a lot of beautiful desert pictures.

In June, Roman was not home one morning. I had to call 911 for an SVT, but the ambulance was given our house number with one incorrect digit. My heart stopped on its own, so I cancelled the ambulance, just minutes before they came. They insisted I go to emergency to get checked over.

In July, I drove solo to Kristin's to do some babysitting for a week. Driving is a challenge for me, especially finding where Kristin and Oless live in rural Mission.

My insomnia is my only problem now, so I chose to see a female psychiatrist in Osoyoos. It is working very well for me.

March 1, 2017, we got to watch three otters on top of our frozen lake. It was very entertaining. We had never seen them before. The otters covered a great distance quickly with small leaps forward and then gliding. They started out in a bay south of our place and travelled north to the entrance of Inkaneep Creek.

When things got too busy or stressful, I would increase my Lithium to 450 mg. When things slow down, I go back to 300 mg. I asked to try Remeron for sleep and insomnia. I took it for over a year until I was fed up with side effects.

It was a very busy year in 2018 for turkey vultures hovering over our property. They are huge, ugly and strange. It has become more common to see them the past few years.

April snowpack was 152 percent of normal. May 10, 11, and 12 were the worst of this year's flood with strong winds causing much more erosion. It was our worst year of flooding since we have owned our farm.

In June, we attended Orysia's first dance concert when she was about five and a half years old. I danced, Kristin danced and now Orysia.

This June/July I got my largest crop of Saskatoon berries. I filled up a freezer shelf. I eat some every day with breakfast. It is very peaceful picking berries along the lakeshore.

August was the worst fire season on record. There was smoke in the air for about five weeks. No proper sunshine for that long has an effect on everyone.

In August, Kristin and Oless, Orysia and Orrin came for their holiday. They stay down at our cabin and thoroughly enjoyed themselves. This year Orysia was able to climb Throne Mountain with Roman and Kristin. Oless was so impressed he decided to climb with Kristin two days later.

This fall was the first time our creek failed to flow. It is a key feature of the north end of our property and my grotto. It is a drainage easement area but the workers for the neighbour have dumped debris there over the past years. Nothing should ever be put in a drainage easement.

In October, I had another SVT and tried different tricks to stop it, waiting two hours before going to emergency. They told me this time not to wait more than half an hour. They got everything hooked up. My heart was at 167, then after 10 minutes it quit on its own. I was tired though for a week.

November 21, my friend Bruce passed away. We met at Braemore Lodge 16 years ago. Three days following, my friend Barbara passed away. She was the identical twin to another friend Pat who died years ago. Pat and Barbara were both great artists. I have their paintings in my home.

Roman left for Arizona in early December 2018. I had planned to start working on my book by January 2. I would be turning 70 on January 28, a very good reason to finish my goal. I'm not a writer or a good speller. The most important thing is that I had a story to tell.

Writing longhand allows the brain to process so much more. Our emotions surface and we feel what we felt way back then. It might have been anger, fear, hurt, or shame. We can be so vulnerable after trauma in our life.

25. Finding Balance

For many years my feelings were suppressed by medications. Coming off medication, I entered a very difficult time in my life.

I was a nice person, but full of anger and often aggressive. Memories from childhood sexual abuse had been repressed. I had minimized my terror and shame as a child and as a patient on the psych ward.

Most of the work in my recovery program has been about self-help. I've had many professionals and counsellors giving advice and guidance along the way.

If a workshop came up in the area, I would attend and enjoy the learning experience. The "Women and Anger" workshop by Margaret Malone in Osoyoos in 1993 was excellent. Through Okanagan College, I took part in a stress workshop, acupressure and reflexology courses.

As abuse issues in my life surfaced, my anger escalated. I did not understand what was happening to me. My physical and emotional health deteriorated. I feared psychiatrists and medical doctors could not help me.

The "Stop the Violence" counselling program was a big step forward for me. I was finally being heard. I also participated in a survivor group.

Over my lifetime, I have seen many doctors, specialists, psychiatrists and counsellors. An emotionally traumatized person can present a rather large mixed bag of complaints and symptoms.

To gain knowledge, I began to go back into my education as a nurse. I picked up books from thrift shops, secondhand bookstores or the library. If the book was highly recommended, I'd buy it and later use it for reference. Councillors gave me helpful handouts and worksheets.

In my teens, I kept diaries, which I still have. They clearly indicate emotional problems of long duration. I have been journaling on a daily basis for most of my life. I've studied and made notes on all areas of health care.

Gaining knowledge of the mind and body connection gave me the power to reclaim my life. It is so true when they say, "Listen to your body."

Becoming an informed patient was empowering. If there's a single lesson from my own experience that I would like to share with readers, it's to become an informed patient and take charge of your own health care. Become proactive and be your own advocate. I am often surprised how many people don't know much about their medications, their blood pressure and other important health issues. My nursing background has helped me to understand the medical language and I've always been interested.

The medical system does not take well to informed patients. It would have been easier to pretend I knew nothing and did not care about my life as a "mentally ill" person. I could have cooperated and continued taking medications as prescribed.

It would be very shocking to know the number and kinds of drugs I have been on over the past 40 years. Medications have their place, but in my case, they blocked normal feelings and emotions. My issues from the past were suppressed by pills to "calm me down."

Unresolved stress is called "distress." I dealt with the pain and fatigue, not knowing it was connected to my childhood, Dr. Anderson or the psych ward. My "distress" took its toll on my physical and emotional health.

Writing allowed me to express feelings, anger, resentments and hurts. It even helped in expressing rage towards my abusers and the people who did not protect me. I was able to have a nice big fire, burning the words and emotions in the burn barrel. It felt so good.

I then had the ability to focus on more positive and creative writing. Healing my spirit was a priority.

I've been big on goalsetting most of my life. I'd be making lists of short-term goals and a few long-term goals. I make many to-do lists and grocery lists. Anything is possible.

One of the biggest motivators is a calendar with daily recordings of weather, social and physical activities and completed projects. I use bright colours to do all my calendars. Years ago when my life was upside down, the calendars were too.

* * *

For me, being outdoors and close to nature has been tremendously healing. I might plan a 20-minute walk and be gone 45 minutes.

My "grotto" by the lake has given me something constructive to do, something peaceful. It's usually quieter in the off-season when there are no noisy speeding boats, particularly in the morning or late evening.

Often the only sound is the call of a loon that sits offshore in the spring and fall.

I used to do a lot of crafts. People would say it's a nice hobby and must be relaxing, but crafts made me really uptight. Especially sewing, because I would take everything so seriously and try to do everything perfectly. But if I'm outside, it doesn't have to be perfect because it's just me. My creativity can be expressed in my natural surroundings.

* * *

The dream catcher is a gift of love and inspiration with roots in various native cultures across North America. They are given to someone you care for in the hope their dreams are fulfilled.

I have three of my own dream catchers. They are specific feathers I collected in nature.

The first one is very tiny. It was made with a small collection of feathers from the Honolulu Zoo. One feather is from the pink flamingo bird. The hoop is only two inches across.

My second creation involved a 19-inch hoop. The feathers are all California quail and pheasant. Tanya, my First Nations friend, was able to show me the correct stringing and tying of the knots. The string is dark brown and the beads all wooden in natural colours.

The last dream catcher is all feathers from a dead bald eagle. I found it on the shore of a lake north of Merritt. I used variegated white to black yarn and white and black beads. I used a nine-inch hoop.

I do many crafts with nature items. It's hard to resist picking up feathers of interest. I had to sort mine, keep the best and throw away the rest. My mallard duck ones will be great.

A hummingbird crashed and died on our deck. I created a card using all of its feathers. Earlier, I had done creative taxidermy on a quail.

It is very sad to see the dream catchers on display in gift shops. Most do not come close to being realistic, with very plain feathers in shades of pink and purple.

* * *

One of the most empowering moments of my life occurred in March 2006. This was two months after Dr. Anderson was sentenced to 18 months jail.

It was going to be a beautiful sunny day. I spontaneously decided to drive to Penticton to do some grocery shopping.

Something else had been on my mind as well. I needed to go to Penticton Regional Hospital. I wanted to speak to the administrator regarding unresolved issues.

First, I looked for the location of the offices. The sign indicated the fourth floor. It wasn't the fourth floor on the first set of elevators. It was the fourth floor on the pink elevators. When I got out, I searched in the maze of offices for one indicating "administrator."

I spoke with a pleasant secretary who kindly offered to ask the administrator if she had time to speak with me. The administrator came to greet me and take me to a quiet room. We sat opposite each other at a small table. She took notes and listened with respect and compassion.

I explained my circumstances regarding Dr. Anderson and the Penticton Hospital back in the 1970s. I told her how I had been abused sexually, emotionally and physically when I was a patient on the psych ward.

I told her how the administration and staff knew about Dr. Anderson's conduct back in 1979. A meeting was held, but I was not invited to come and speak on my behalf as his patient of nine years. At that time, several staff members on psych suggested I should sue the hospital. I was on too many drugs to figure anything out that complicated.

My intention in visiting the administrator was to request some sort of acknowledgement or validation. I said that six years of work getting

Dr. Anderson convicted was stressful for all of us women. His punishment did not suit the crimes.

"The three women who were witnesses were just the tip of the iceberg," I said.

I did break down and cry. I always hurt when I tell how they took my baby away. I said I did get her back though and I proudly added that she had just graduated with her Master's in economics.

That day I felt like I had taken charge and was empowered. I was going to make the hospital accountable. I did not want to sue or go to court. I just wanted someone to be accountable for what happened and express remorse.

A few months later, in June 2006, I received a letter from Kim Marshall, director of Mental Health and Addictions for the Okanagan Health Service Area following up on my meeting with Lorraine Ferguson, community administrator for South Okanagan.

The letter acknowledged that Dr. Anderson's behaviour with clients had just been dealt with in the courts. My complaint about physical abuse by one of the employees in the psych ward could not be followed up because he was no longer an employee and some 30 years had passed.

"... We believe that advances have been made over the last 20 to 30 years in patient care techniques, such that the care is often more respectful now than was the standard in the past," she wrote. "... Although knowledge of current practices may not change your remembrance of the care you received in the past, we hope it provides you with comfort to know that advances have been made."

The letter, of course, couldn't undo the damage. But I felt good because these people were finally admitting that they weren't doing their job and they needed to be accountable for what happened to me and the other women who were abused by Dr. Anderson and some of the other staff.

I felt better and never had any desire to go back to administration and deal with them again. I felt like I'd finally been allowed to speak and say what I had to say. I have the letter as proof that I actually did that, and it felt good.

* * *

I am now on greatly reduced medications. A small dose of lithium (150 mg) will lower the amount of norepinephrine in my brain, which can trigger fight or flight mode.

I've been on lithium a total of 30 years in my lifetime. The higher doses recommended for a bipolar disorder never helped me at all.

For chronic complex PTSD, a low dose is effective for episodes of inappropriate anger, irritability, anxiety and insomnia.

My most recent experience on lithium has been the past 10 years. I gradually lowered my dose from 600 mg, 450 mg, 300 mg and now 150 mg. With additional stress I can increase the dose.

I used to tell my psychiatrists that I was either "wired" or "tired." It was not "manic or depressed" as they assumed.

A lower dose of lithium also causes far fewer side effects than doses of 900 mg to 1,800 mg used for bipolar.

My only other medication is Clonazepam, a very potent benzodiazepine. Used with caution, it is a strong antianxiety drug.

I'm a much happier person now. My obsessive thoughts are much more controllable. I'm much calmer and I don't think things get me fired up like they used to. I used to get very angry. That's typical as anger is a big part of post-traumatic stress, coming from fear as a child.

Just as my father's anger settled down as he grew older, I too believe I've found peace.

I think a lesson from my experience is that you can be a survivor, even if you have gone through life and it looks like you'll never survive what you went through. It's been a long journey to get here.

One councillor told me that I'm not just a survivor. "You're a thriver," she said.

* * *

Down the steep trail to the water's edge in my "grotto," I arrange some driftwood, shells from Hawaii, rocks from Oregon and ceramic angels from Sandy and Diane.

A kingfisher sits in the tall poplars above me. Nesting mergansers, grebes, mallards and coots are raising their families along the shoreline. They are protected by tall reeds.

I reflect on the beauty around me. Despite all the memories of what has happened in my life, memories that will never completely be erased, this is a special place. I've not only survived, but I am stronger.

Appendix – Glossary of Medications and Medical Terms

Ativan – (lorazepam) is a benzodiazepine medication used to treat anxiety disorders, insomnia and other conditions.

Benzodiazepine – a class of psychoactive drugs used in treating anxiety, insomnia and agitation. Among early benzodiazepines were Valium and Librium. They are considered minor tranquilizers.

Bipolar disorder – Once called "manic depression," bipolar disorder causes periods of depression and at other times elevated moods known as "mania" when the person feels energetic, happy or irritable and may make poor decisions.

BMR – basal metabolic rate – This is the rate of energy expenditure by time in people or animals at rest. BMR is the rate at which someone burns calories and affects whether they gain or lose weight. It is affected by the thyroid and by drugs used to treat hyperthyroidism.

CAT scan (or CT scan - computerized axial tomography) – These are special X-ray images taken at different angles and combined by a computer process to create cross-sectional images of the scanned area in the body.

Chlorpromazine – Chlorpromazine is an antipsychotic medication sold as Thorazine and Largactil. It is used to treat schizophrenia and the manic phase of bipolar disorder among other conditions.

Clonazepam – Sold as Klonopin and under other names, this medication is used to prevent and treat seizures and panic disorder. It is a benzodiazepine class drug.

ECT – electroconvulsive therapy treatments used to electrically induce seizures to provide relief for major depressive disorder, mania and catatonia. Common side effects are confusion and temporary memory loss.

Electrocardiogram (ECG) – An electrocardiogram is a test to check the function of the heart by measuring its electrical activity.

Eliquis – (apixaban) is an anticoagulant (blood thinner) used to treat and prevent blood clots and prevent strokes in people with certain heart conditions such as atrial fibrillation.

Endocrine – The endocrine system releases hormones through internal glands such as the thyroid and adrenal glands.

Epival – Epival is one of the valproic acid drugs used as an anticonvulsant and antimanic drug as well as for migraines. It is often used to treat epilepsy and manic episodes resulting from bipolar disorder.

Haldol – (haloperidol) is an antipsychotic medication used for the treatment of schizophrenia and mania of bipolar disorder.

Hyperthyroidism – An overactive thyroid can occur when a person's thyroid gland produces too much thyroxine, the thyroid hormone. It can result in irritability, muscle weakness, sleeping problems, a fast heartbeat, heat intolerance and weight loss.

Hypnotism – The inducement of hypnosis, an enhanced capacity to respond to suggestion. It is used as hypnotherapy for therapeutic purposes but is also used as stage hypnosis by mentalists as a form of entertainment.

Hypothyroidism – Hypothyroidism is an endocrine disorder in which the thyroid gland doesn't produce enough thyroid hormone. It can result in low tolerance of cold, tiredness, depression and weight gain. Too little iodine in the diet can be a major cause, but it can result from a defective thyroid or, in Bonnie's case, from over prescription of drugs to treat misdiagnosed hyperthyroidism. Lithium can also cause hypothyroidism.

INR (international normalized ratio) – The prothrombin time is used to determine the clotting tendency of blood and is used to measure the impact of Warfarin dosage. INR is used to standardize the results of this test.

IUD – intrauterine device, a coil or t-shaped birth control device that is inserted into a woman's uterus to prevent pregnancy.

Lamictal – (lamotrigine) is an anticonvulsant medication used to treat epilepsy and bipolar disorder.

Lithium – Lithium is a psychiatric medication often used to treat bipolar disorder as well as other psychiatric conditions.

LPN – licensed practical nurse

Manic – A state of abnormally elevated arousal and heightened energy. The heightened mood can be either euphoric or irritable. It can result in a flight of ideas, decreased need for sleep, and hyperactivity.

Manic-depressive – see Bipolar disorder above.

Norepinephrine – (noradrenalin) is a naturally occurring chemical in the body that functions in the brain and body as a hormone and neurotransmitter. It mobilizes the brain and body for action, and it is produced at a higher level in situations of stress or danger in the "fight-or-flight" response.

Paxil – (paroxetine) is an antidepressant medication in the SSRI (selective serotonin reuptake inhibitor) family, which also includes such drugs as Prozac and Zoloft.

Pedophilia – A psychiatric disorder in which an older person is sexually attracted to children.

Phlebitis – inflammation of a vein, usually in the legs.

Propylthiouracil – is a medication used to manage hyperthyroidism, which is due to an overactive thyroid gland. It decreases the amount of thyroid hormone.

PTSD – Post-traumatic stress disorder – This is a mental disorder that can result from a person being exposed to a traumatic event such as a sexual assault, war, major accident or other threats to a person's life. It can alter how a person thinks and feels and increase the "fight-or-flight" response.

Remeron – (mirtazapine) is an antidepressant used to treat depression. It tends to begin being effective sooner than the SSRI class of antidepressant. Sometimes it can help insomnia.

Restoril – (temazepam) is used to treat insomnia. It is an intermediate benzodiazepine and hypnotic. It can cause dependence and so is generally used as a short-term drug.

RN – registered nurse

Schizophrenia – A mental illness resulting in separation from reality, for example hearing voices that don't exist.

Seroquel – (quetiapine) is used to treat schizophrenia, bipolar disorder and major depressive disorder. It is widely used as a sleep aid, but it is not recommended for this purpose.

Straitjacket – A straitjacket is a garment with extra-long sleeves that can be tied together to restrain the arms of a mental patient. Their use is considered antiquated and they are now rarely used in psychiatric hospitals. The feet are restrained separately.

Supraventricular tachycardia (SVT) – This is an abnormally fast heart rhythm due to malfunctioning electrical activity in the upper part of the heart. Paroxysmal supraventricular tachycardia (PSVT) is a form which can result in a heart rhythm between 150 and 240 beats per minute. It can be triggered by psychological stress.

Thyroid – The thyroid gland is an endocrine gland in the neck. The three hormones it produces affect the metabolic rate and protein synthesis. See also Hypothyroidism and Hyperthyroidism above.

Trazodone – Trazodone is an antidepressant medication used to treat major depressive and anxiety disorders. It also has sedating properties and is used as an alternative to benzodiazepines to treat insomnia.

Warfarin – is used as a blood thinner or anticoagulant often to treat blood clots and to prevent strokes in people with certain heart conditions. It can cause bleeding as a side effect. Its original use was as a rat poison.

Xanax – (alprazolam) is a short-acting benzodiazepine used to manage anxiety and panic disorders.

Zoloft – (sertraline) is an antidepressant medication in the SSRI (selective serotonin reuptake inhibitor) family, which also includes such drugs as Prozac and Paxil.

Zopiclone – Zopiclone is a nonbenzodiazepine hypnotic used to treat insomnia. It tranquilizes the central nervous system. It can result in withdrawal symptoms when stopped abruptly.

Zyprexa – (olanzapine) is an antipsychotic medication used to treat bipolar disorder and schizophrenia.